Students in Trouble

Schools Can Help before Failure

William L. Fibkins

ScarecrowEducation
Lanham, Maryland • Toronto • Oxford
2005

LB1620.5
.F477
2005

o 57168126

Published in the United States of America
by ScarecrowEducation
An imprint of The Rowman & Littlefield Publishing Group, Inc.
4501 Forbes Boulevard, Suite 200, Lanham, Maryland 20706
www.scaroweducation.com

PO Box 317
Oxford
OX2 9RU, UK

Copyright © 2005 by William L. Fibkins

All rights reserved. No part of this publication may be reproduced,
stored in a retrieval system, or transmitted in any form or by any
means, electronic, mechanical, photocopying, recording, or otherwise,
without the prior permission of the publisher.

British Library Cataloguing in Publication Information Available

Library of Congress Cataloging-in-Publication Data

Fibkins, William L.
  Students in trouble : schools can help before failure / William L. Fibkins.
    p. cm.
  Includes bibliographical references and index.
  ISBN 1-57886-246-9 (pbk. : alk. paper)
  1. Counseling in secondary education—United States. 2. School failure—
United States—Prevention. 3. Behavior modification—United States. I. Title.
LB1620.5.F48 2005
373.14—dc22

2004027797

∞™ The paper used in this publication meets the minimum requirements of
American National Standard for Information Sciences—Permanence of Paper
for Printed Library Materials, ANSI/NISO Z39.48-1992.
Manufactured in the United States of America.

Contents

Acknowledgments

This book is dedicated to my wife, Kathy Fibkins. She has been a steady source of support throughout my various projects, projects that sometimes met great resistance and were difficult at best. Her counsel and encouraging words have helped me put forward my best efforts and maintain the will to win, even when doubts and possible failures loomed. As this book suggests, she has provided a wonderful open door that I can pass through when I, like many students, need an advisor who listens, cares, and provides hope and possibilities.

Thanks, Kathy, for all you do and are.

1

Students in Trouble

The major premise of this book is to challenge the ways schools label and respond to students who are experiencing difficulties in their school lives. As I point out in my book *An Educator's Guide to Understanding the Personal Side of Students' Lives*, more and more adolescents are coming to school with personal and well-being problems.[1] These problems can have a negative impact on their learning process, social and emotional adjustment, and healthy development, sometimes leading to life-long battles to overcome eating disorders, such as anorexia, bulimia, or obesity, and addictions to tobacco, alcohol, and drugs. These emotional and physical problems are of great concern to the students themselves and their parents who need guidance and training on how to intervene to help their children.

In my experience as an educator, I have found that most students want to succeed. When they meet roadblocks in their learning and personal development, they want to resolve these issues. However, we need to keep in mind that many students do not know how to ask for help when they become troubled. The process of connecting with a caring adult who will invite them to talk and then being able to speak openly about their struggle with a serious family illness or divorce or problem with finding their niche in a new school doesn't come easily for adolescents already experiencing disruption in their school and family lives.

Some students have multiple disruptions that can thrust them too soon out of adolescence into an adult role they are not prepared for. These students begin to develop a point of view that "this is the way it is." Finding an open door to walk through for help doesn't exist. Help is not on the way.

I believe this is the reality for many students headed toward trouble in the schools. In a sense they are savvy and don't hold out much hope of an encounter with a caring adult who will help them successfully navigate through these tough times. They know that the current intervention practice in many schools is focused on a small number of what are called "troubled students," a minority of students labeled as acting out, lazy, slackers, bullies, resistant to learning, uncooperative, truants, and class cutters.

These students may have bad reputations and poor school histories; be from "bad" families; abuse tobacco, drugs, or alcohol; and stir up trouble for teachers and administrators. These students are often labeled "at risk" and receive a great deal of attention and the energy of administrators, counselors, school psychologists, social workers, teachers, and support staff—attention that has a counseling component but often results in detention and suspension. As these students miss more and more class time, they drift into a cycle of acting out, suspension, reentry to school, followed by more acting out, and for many, expulsion or dropping out.

This is particularly true for students addicted to tobacco, alcohol, or drugs, who cannot go through the school day without a cigarette, a drink, or drugs. Often their daily routine is to be tardy, cut class, and search out unsupervised areas to hang out. In the end, as principal Barbara Reis Wager recalls in her early experience as a school principal, it is clear that suspension doesn't work.[2] The fact is that teachers defensively rationalize a system that no longer works. Crippled by the apparently unsolvable problems, they rely on suspension like a crutch.

What's wrong with this process? Plenty! It saps the energy, time, skills, and sometimes the spirit from dedicated and caring educators who often see their intervention efforts result in failure. After all, a student who is suspended or expelled, or who drops out of school represents a failure for educators, the student, the parents, and the community who must search for a positive way to salvage this student's life. And it is a failure process for the majority of students and parents who are experiencing problems but find themselves left out of the school's intervention loop where help is available only for at-risk students. By focusing most of our intervention resources and efforts on the "troubled" child—the acting out, at-risk student—I argue that we have failed to attend to the "child in trouble," the majority of students who are trying to navigate through the emotional, social, and well-being problems that occur in adolescent development.

I believe that as educators we need to begin to change our frame of reference to include an ongoing assessment of each child and be prepared to offer intervention when needed. This includes the best and brightest, who often shield their problems, and their parents, who are often focused only on achievement and may miss the signs of problems caused by the ongoing pressure that comes with being labeled "gifted" and a "rising star."

We must intervene early on to help parents like Lewis and Mary Ann, characters in author Tom Perrotto's book *All the Children Are above Average*. Mary Ann likes to remind her four-year-old that he is going to Harvard.[3] Lewis, in an effort to put an end to this too-early pressure, finally reacts and says, "Our son is four years old; you have to stop talking to him about Harvard."

We must move away from the perception that only a small minority of so-called at-risk students, who dominate the time and conversation of staff, students, and parents, need intervention, and move away from the narrowly defined labels such as at risk that stigmatize students and keep educators focused on only this small percentage of the school population.

This issue does not command the attention of education reformers in the same way as reducing the size of our secondary schools, class size, and raising test scores, but it has, in my opinion, the possibility to make significant changes in our schools that will help children without entailing a major overhaul. The recent interest in the programs to leave no child behind has opened a needed discussion aimed at broadening the definition of which children receive intervention in the schools. As Children's Defense Fund President Marian Wright Edelman suggests, this requires ensuring that every child has what he or she needs to be healthy, safe, and cared for in order to learn and providing successful passage to adulthood with the help of caring families and communities.[4]

Clearly, increasing the educational attainment of every child, leaving no child behind, is one of our nation's highest priorities. As the Centers for Disease Control and Prevention (CDC) report, everyone wants students to succeed. Parents want their children to do well in school to ensure a self-sufficient, happy future.[5] Colleges and universities want applicants who are well prepared and serious about learning. Businesses want productive,

well-trained, motivated workers. Perhaps most of all, the school community wants students to succeed, to fulfill its education mission. However,
amid calls for smaller classrooms and improved teacher training to increase test scores, a key piece of the education equation is often overlooked: the emotional, social, and physical well-being of the students.

I strongly agree with this assessment. Having served as an education re-
former, teacher trainer, psychologist, and counselor at the middle school,
junior high, and high school levels, I know firsthand how important the
emotional, social, and physical well-being of students is to their academic
success. I also know from my own experience in developing teacher advisory, counseling, student peer helper and leadership, support staff, and
parent training programs that addressing the recommendations of the
CDC is doable given the adoption of new ways to focus on intervention.

Michele Cahill, a senior counselor for education policy for the New
York City schools, calls for changes in student support services to bring
about greater personal attention for students in an example of school leaders beginning to rethink how best to address the growing nonacademic
needs of adolescents.[6] That means, as I suggest, beginning to view teens
who develop personal and well-being problems as children headed for
trouble rather than troubled children.

I believe troubled children is a negative label that suggests children
who have something wrong with them. A more positive and helpful approach is suggested by author and educator Chris Mercogliano, who reports, "We don't consider that certain kids have something wrong. Some
kids are more energetic, more distractible; some kids are angrier than others."[7] Mercogliano also addresses one of the core reasons why some students are labeled as troubled when he suggests, "Public schools are under
so much pressure that kids who don't readily fit in, that don't get with the
program and sit still and cooperate, are big problems." The label children
headed for trouble is much more comprehensive, inclusive, and positive,
suggesting that all children at some point in their education career can run
into difficulty in school, and skilled educators, in concert with families,
can intervene to redirect these students in a positive direction. This
process opens up many doors of help for students and their parents, providing them with hope, skills, and confidence.

However, I argue in this book that the majority of secondary schools in
America are simply not organized to respond to the growing number of

troubled students and parents affected by personal and well-being problems and the alienation and anonymity that often accompany these problems. They are not ready for the task of leaving no child behind when it comes to intervention on personal and well-being problems. Why? First and foremost is the limited mission and vision of many secondary schools when it comes to intervening to help students heading for trouble.

The reality of school life for many caring and concerned school administrators, counselors, teacher leaders, and parents is that they are operating within a student intervention system that is flawed and out of date, a system that serves only to sidetrack their efforts to respond to students and parents heading toward the margins of school life and into trouble. I believe these educators on the front lines of our secondary schools need a road map to determine how they can reorganize their intervention system and be freed at last to address these issues. This book, then, is also about how educators can proceed to make an honest assessment and fundamental changes in the way they currently envision and deliver counseling and health-related services; develop an expanded definition of which students need intervention, not merely the students labeled as troubled, tough, or at risk; and how to proceed to create a schoolwide support environment and team that enlists teachers, students, support staff, parents, and administrators as creditable and easily available sources of help, support, and guidance — an intervention system that leaves no child or parent behind and a system that leaves no caring administrator, counselor, teacher, support staff, student, or parent behind, deprived of the necessary training, skills, and tools to be of help and use to every student in the school community.

It necessitates a team of collective helpers ready and set to respond to an ever-changing student population who arrive each day at the schoolhouse door with a variety of needs, values, hope, and dreams, and, yes, fears of failure and not belonging.

Yet honest assessments are often difficult. As organizations and as persons we tend to go with what we know even when we see our daily efforts mired in failure. This phenomenon can be seen in our schools very clearly in the continuing and flawed process of relying on a few guidance counselors to resolve the growing number of students' problems.

Maybe this system worked well in the 1950s when there were fewer students, a more stable family and community life, and employment opportunities and enlistment in the armed services for poorly performing students which did not require a high school diploma or college degree. There were many more open doors for students encountering problems in their school life through which they could exit with honor and dignity. They had a valid destination and could find their niche outside the school-house. In the eyes of their parents and community members, they were not dropouts, but kids choosing another path. As a result, the schools did not have to build an effective student intervention system that had the capacity to meet the needs of changing student populations, culture, economics, and family/community life.

But as the reader knows, times have changed—dramatically. Our secondary schools are larger, some with enrollments of 2,500 students. Student mobility is on the rise. *Education Week* reports that the 2000 U.S. Census found that 15 to 20 percent of school-aged children had moved in the previous year. A U.S. General Accounting Office 1994 study found one out of six children had attended three or more schools by the end of third grade.[8] Student, parent, and staff anonymity and alienation can flourish in this kind of environment. It is easy for teens to move through six years of middle school, junior high, and high school without being known or noticed.

It is easy to go down wrong roads and get lost. Researchers Roberta G. Simmons and Dale A. Blyth report that students can be thrust too soon out of childhood into adolescence before they are ready for the change.[9] Simmons and Blyth also report that there are negative consequences for adolescents who must cope with several transitions at once. Girls suffer losses in self-esteem when the number of life-change events they are exposed to increases. Both males and females exhibit declines in GPA and extracurricular participation the more of these transitions they encounter. Facing multiple life changes simultaneously has deleterious effects on young adolescents.

And our school population is more diverse. Schools face a growing number of immigrant newcomers to our country and communities who look for assistance on how to fit in, learn, and find their niche. Children of same-sex couples are part of this growing diversity. And high-stakes testing puts new pressure on school staff, students, and parents. The pressure on students and parents for admittance into the best colleges continues to mount. For example, the *New York Times* reports that in 2002 private student tutoring services took in 3.5 billion dollars as more students and parents sought academic help outside the school environment.[10]

The emphasis on participating in sports as a way to win a scholarship to play Division 1 athletics also brings added pressure for students, parents, and educators. The *New York Times* reported that forty million children participate in organized sports in the United States, a cultural phenomenon known as much for its excesses as for its successes.[11] Tales of overburdened children playing sports out of season, of demands to specialize in a single sport as early as grade school, of competitive pressures that lead to national championships for nine-year-olds—even in something like power lifting. "The shame of it is you see how hardened these 14-year-olds are by the time they get to high school," said Bruce Ward, director of physical education and athletics in San Diego's schools. "They're talented, terrific players, but I don't see the joy. They look tired. They've played so much year round, they are like little professionals."

Reporter Margaret Talbot suggests child prodigies are more common in all sports than they were even ten years ago.[12] They may be more common because parents start their kids in formal lessons at earlier ages, or because there are more sports to choose from and therefore a greater chance that kids will find one at which they turn out to be remarkable. The Sporting Goods Manufacturers Association, which ten years ago tracked participation trends in 60 sports, now tracks 103, including new extreme sports.

It comes as no surprise that this highly competitive culture in which many students and parents use sports as a way to get ahead, has its excesses and down sides. Writer Darcy Frey, reporting about the dashed hopes of New York City's Lincoln High School basketball stars Tchaka Shipp, Cory Johnson, and Darryle Flicking to play basketball in the National Basketball Association, reminds us of relying too heavily on sports to get ahead.[13] She reports that each year 500,000 or so young men play high school basketball in this country. Each year less than 1 percent of them get a Division 1 scholarship. The bitter disappointments of players like Shipp, Johnson, and Flicking are the norm but you wouldn't know it from reading the sports pages or from tuning to ESPN. There is the myth of basketball as the great way to thrive, uncomplicated by the stories of the young men who never made it. Those players are quickly forgotten, left to show up at the playgrounds, where they curl their fingers around the chain-link fencing and peer at their younger selves out there on the asphalt, wondering what happened to them at such a tender age in their lives.

The *Washington Post* reported on a scandal that stunned Howard County, Maryland, a highly ranked school system, that included grade tampering at Columbia Oakland Mills High School that resulted in the football team's forfeiting a spot in the state playoffs.[14] In all, sixteen athletes and cheerleaders were found to be academically ineligible. Reporter Timothy Egan echoes another negative aspect of the students' seeking an advantage in the highly competitive world of high school sports when he reports that more than ever, American boys are trying to find designer bodies not just in a gym but in a syringe of illegal steroids or a bottle of legal equivalent in a local nutrition store.[15] Nearly half a million teenagers in the United States use steroids each year.

In Clearfield, Utah, about forty miles north of Salt Lake City, the school has built a large weight room. The principal, Mike Timothy, said he could sometimes tell which students were using steroids or precursors not because their appearance had changed so dramatically but because they were also quick-tempered. It's called "roid" rage. "Suddenly you've got some kids who are ready to fight at the drop of a hat," said Mr. Timothy. And then there is a growing health problem in the increased use of antidepressant drugs for students that is often accompanied by aggressive, violent, and suicidal behavior. The *New York Times* reports about eleven million prescriptions for a group of newer antidepressants written for children under the age of eighteen in 2002 in the United States.[16]

All of these issues are demanding the attention of administrators who are already overwhelmed responding to at-risk students. Faced with the reality that they are boxed in by an antiquated intervention system, many of these administrators are looking for new approaches that will enable them to move beyond only responding to these at-risk students, the negative stars of the school, and creating new intervention to help every student. They seek new approaches that will serve to broaden the intervention vision of staff, students, and parents, and shift their attention, commitment, and helping skills away from their narrow focus on acting-out students who dominate the negative conversations in faculty rooms, student lunch rooms, and PTA meetings to proactive responses that enlist their spirit of caring.

The school environment then is often hectic and goal oriented for students, parents, and staff except for the acting-out, at-risk students and those students encountering learning, personal, and well-being problems that cause them to drift quietly, unnoticed, to the margins of school life. The culture is focused on the future—getting into the best colleges, winning scholarships, achieving the highest test scores, claiming the county sports titles, and so on. As such, it's a school environment that can foster alienation and anonymity for the majority of students who show up each day not wearing the label of at risk or standard-bearer.

While many of these students may be experiencing personal and well-being problems that impact negatively on their learning, they exist quietly, in the vast middle, their troubles hidden except for clues such as a bruised face caused by abuse, a sudden lackluster school performance, little or no parent involvement, continuing health-related problems with increased time spent in the nurse's office, and so on. And it is also an environment in which it is easy for many staff members to become alienated and anonymous, not called upon to be an adult model, mentor, or source of help for students.

In a real sense what we have created is a school environment in which it is difficult for every student and parent to ask for help when they encounter personal and well-being problems that interfere with their learning and development. As Thomas Fowler-Finn, superintendent of the Fort Wayne (Indiana) Community Schools, suggests, improving achievement involves much more than taking measures to raise test scores. It also involves understanding our students' perceptions, how they view their educators and education, and a host of other things. He argues that fostering real achievement may also depend on expanding our definition of what achievement means.[17] If we want all students to achieve, not just on tests but in their lives, trying to understand as best we can who they are and where they are coming from may be the best place to start.

For example, the standard-bearers, those students who star in academics, sports, the arts and music, and the like, often view themselves and are viewed by school staff and parents as problem free. They are not allowed to have problems. That is, they can't miss school; not be on the honor roll; not perform well in sports, music, and theater; not cut class; not turn in assignments; not act out; not raise their hands or have the right answer; and so on. In other words, they can't just be. Their guiding principle is, "If you have problems, keep them to yourself." They are bothered by the pressure of college admissions and taking four advanced placement courses, sick, literally, of keeping weight down as star wrestlers, tired of the never-ending summer camps and weekend traveling teams to help get noticed by Division 1 coaches, and taking part in all those school activities to help inflate their college applications.

Suppose they want to jump off the pressure bandwagon? Not easy. Key words are don't show staff, peers, and sometimes your parents that, yes, you are human and can experience tough times. Don't let the cracks show through so they need to take notice of you as a person. You hope your peers, parents, and teachers will ignore your shaking hands, the extra beers you're downing on weekends, and the anger and envy you have toward those students who act out and have no expectations for themselves except just to exist. Oh, the wish to be just like them, at least for a day, and experience no pressures, no deadlines, and no demands, just be able to hang out and be a kid.

However, the chosen role for most high achievers is to be a good soldier, keep your mouth shut, and take pride in your numbers—high test scores, batting average, and class rank. Take pride in reports of your achievements in the local paper and save the clippings for your parents' scrapbook. Take pride that you are probably going to get a "full ride" to Princeton. You can live and enjoy life later on. Keep the numbers moving up. Keep the lid on your anxiety. All this work will be worth it later on, so they say. Defer, defer. But watch out if you're an achieving student who sees his or her numbers drop and becomes suddenly aware that even with all your hard work you may still be out of the running.

Who is to help this child? Remember the message in the 2002 film *Better Luck Tomorrow*, by Justin Lin, about a group of Asian American high school students in Orange County, California, who started by selling exam answers and ended up involved in drugs and murder without getting caught. In the original ending of the film when it played at Sundance, the central character considers turning himself in to the police but, "I couldn't let one mistake get in the way of everything I'd worked for. I know the difference between right and wrong, but I guess in the end I really wanted to go to a good college."[18] Exaggeration? Can't happen in my school? Maybe. But pressure to succeed can have its downside and cause a gifted student to head toward the margins, looking for a way out.

Let's return to Bruce Ward. The same tired, hardened look, devoid of joy, can also be seen on the faces of gifted and talented academic students who have spent their childhood and adolescence achieving. The reality is that some students run out of energy and motivation. They falter. Learning becomes work with no time out for fun. As educators we need to shine the light of care on our high achievers and make sure these hardworking children are not left behind.

As I have suggested, it is also difficult for those students who don't command the attention of staff by being high achievers or by acting out to ask for help as they run into personal, family, and well-being problems. As one student told me:

> Who cares? I'm invisible. You see, I'm not one of those at-risk kids. I don't go around starting trouble. Those are the kids who get all the attention here. And I'm not a prep, jock, or artsy kid. I don't make the honor roll, play sports, do the theater thing, or get my name in the school paper. God help the preps and jocks if they ever had a life and real problems like me. They'd fold. I'm sick of it all. I'm taking five courses, not a model student, but I do OK, work part time to help my mom as my dad doesn't send the alimony he's supposed to, and take care of my little brother and sister so my mom can get out on weekends with her new boyfriend. But nobody in school asks how I'm doing. I have so many different feelings about my dad, the divorce, my mom dating again, and why I have to take care of my brother and sister all the time. I have no life. Sure, I would love to talk to a teacher or counselor about "me." I'm a nobody. No one is going to call me in for a conference. You know why? Because I don't look like I have problems and I don't act out. Like I say, I'm a nobody. I don't matter here.

As educators we need to shine the light of care on those quiet students who need attention, not leave them behind, turn our heads, because they don't demand our attention or screech out for help. These students are looking for an invitation from a concerned teacher or counselor, such as, "How are you doing today? How's the divorce coming? I know you have a lot going on with going to school, working part time, and caring for your brother and sister. Mike and Joan are their names, right? Let's plan to meet fifth period and talk. It's always confusing when parents are divorcing."

In a unique way, it is hard for the so-called at-risk students to get the help they need, learn new behaviors, and become successful learners. As I have reported earlier in this chapter, every school has its list of at-risk students. This at-risk phenomenon is not new to the schools. As author and educator Cynthia Lightfoot reports, at the time our society began to take note of adolescents and their groups in the early 1900s, the eyes of educators turned quickly to their misbehaviors.[19] Large boys in particular attracted much attention. They were widely recognized as being high spirited, reckless, difficult to control, overconfident, and inclined to drop out of school. Teachers were called upon to address the special problems presented by those of their pupils who were in that awkward place between childhood and adulthood.

This labeling continues today with at-risk students often viewed by staff, peers, and sometimes their own parents as passing time in school and at poor risk for graduation and success in life. At-risk students tend to be grouped by educators and as a result socialize and hang out together. They have spent time together in detention rooms, the principal's office, and in the community after suspension. Their ongoing actions in resisting learning, breaking school rules, and confronting authority often lead to ongoing suspensions. These ongoing suspensions have the negative impact of providing these students with more and more unsupervised time absent of caring mentors and effective intervention programs. Often these suspensions involve smoking on school grounds.

The CDC reports that every day nearly 3,000 young people start smoking. Tobacco use among teens headed toward the margins of school life does provide temporary physical and emotional relief from their negative school experience and ongoing battles with teachers, peers, and administrators. Smoking during school hours does serve as a way, albeit negative, for many unhappy and failing students to connect with other acting-out peers, to be noticed, to be somebody and a part of a group, and to not be alone. Any reader who is a smoker or has smoked knows tobacco works to quell anxiety. The nicotine does temporarily reduce anxiety and provide a moment of calm, as does the use of alcohol and other drugs. Many student smokers are involved in multiple addictions and as a result of their growing addiction are often tardy, truant, and chronic class cutters. Poor nutrition and related health problems are common side effects of these addictions.

Student tobacco use and accompanying behaviors often make up the bulk of discipline issues in many secondary schools. Suspending, detaining, and expelling student smokers are time-consuming tasks for busy administrators. Furthermore, this process does little to help students who want to stop smoking. Yes, many at-risk students get attention, but the attention is often focused on removing these students from the school setting, sometimes for over a month out of each year. The National Center for Education Statistics reports school principals ranked student tardiness and student absenteeism/class cutting first and second among violence and discipline issues in U.S. public schools.[20] Student tobacco use ranked fourth. Clearly one can make the case that student tobacco use leads to tardiness, absenteeism, and class cutting. And of course, being unsupervised and absent from class provides students with fertile ground for developing other addictions and poor health habits.

Suspending and expelling students can result in driving students off campus, where they become vulnerable to negative role models. As researchers Robert L. Sinclair and Ward J. Ghory suggest, if actions are taken to compel the student to "fit in," the conflict between the learner and the school will likely mount.[21] Sometimes the students become less willing to meet demands for compliance. In these cases it is easier for the student to connect with life on the margins, where there is an acceptance of the behaviors the school cannot condone. The distance between the learner and the school widens as positions harden. The way to close the gap is unclear, especially if the school focuses on minimum expectations and does not explore ways to create possibilities for productive connections. Therefore, as educators we need to shine a new kind of light on acting-out students and provide interventions that help them begin to manage their behaviors and addictions so they can return to the classroom and be present mentally and physically, ready to learn, not be left behind, stuck in a world of addictions, poor choices, and a growing loss of hope and belonging.

The number of films on adolescents heading for trouble, such as *Prozac Nation*, *Thirteen*, and *Elephant*, suggest a growing awareness that more and more teenagers are heading toward trouble. They suggest that there is a growing disconnect, malaise, among many teens, resulting in taking risks that endanger their health and sometimes their lives. For example, the film *Prozac Nation* provides a disturbing picture of a depressed young woman who begins cutting herself with a razor blade at the age of twelve and then turns to drugs and alcohol.[22] As educator Michelle Galley reports, student self-harm is a silent school crisis.[23] Young people who intentionally harm themselves, typically by cutting open their skin, are physically acting out extreme emotional distress. Experts say the behavior is becoming more prevalent among teenagers, forcing administrators, teachers, and other school staff members to confront the disturbing issue.

"It is a subtle and private act," said Geoff McKee, the principal of the 1,800 student Boca Raton High School in Florida, "and that is frightening because it can easily go unnoticed." Mr. McKee had never heard of "cutters" until he became a principal five years ago and his school nurse told him about the phenomenon. Since then he has known at least twenty adolescents who purposely injure themselves. Even so, cutting is not a topic of conversation among administrators. Mr. McKee said, "I've never discussed it with another principal and I've never heard it discussed in a professional setting." Experts estimate that upward of 4 percent of adolescents in the United States purposely hurt themselves in some way. That means in a 1,000-student high school, some forty students intentionally harm themselves. This behavior generally starts around age twelve to thirteen.

The film *Thirteen* follows Tracy, its young central figure, as she strays into sex, drugs, and alienation and her sudden detachment from Melanie, her struggling single mother. As film critic Elvis Mitchell suggests, Tracy is acting out a kind of rebelling that doesn't make any sense to her mother.[24] It is the sensation of doing whatever she pleases that both stokes and horrifies her. Melanie recognizes what appears to be her child but doesn't have the tools to get through to her. Tracy is all vivacity looking for boundaries, and Melanie can't provide her daughter with any. Their relationship has been more about acting as friends than parent and offspring. Tracy vibrates those flashes of rage that erupt from the hearts of young girls growing up without a father in the house—a boiling mélange of anger and frustration born of what feels like rejection.

The film *Elephant* details a high school shooting spree modeled on the shootings at Columbine High School at Littleton, Colorado.[25] A *Rolling Stone* review suggests the film's director, Gus Van Sant, sees with piercing clarity the bruises that come from being young in America. Van Sant looks closely at the problems no one, at school or at home, is noticing. For example, tow-headed John McFarland, being driven to school by his drunk father, must take the wheel himself, call his brother for help, and then get detention from a clueless principal. What drove two students, Alex and Eric, to enter school dressed in camouflage gear and carrying guns and to begin shooting? Did anyone wonder why parents, teachers, and peers never noticed what made these two boys outsiders in the first place? Did they wonder when it became so easy for them not to pay attention? It is a film that gets at the small things that can drain a heart of feeling. The film's purpose is to warn us not to turn a blind eye.

The same message of teenagers being disconnected from their families, school, and community is supported in the report "Adrift in America," by Michael D. Resnick, sociologist and professor of pediatrics at the University of Minnesota. This report, featured in the PBS *Frontline* program "The Lost Children of Rockdale County,"[26] explored how a 1996 syphilis outbreak in a well-to-do Atlanta suburb affected more than 200 teenagers and revealed their hidden lives of group sex, binge drinking, drugs, and violence. Resnick reports:

> It's hard to view a story that is so starkly told. We heard a lot about emptiness: houses that were empty and devoid of supervision, adult presence, and oversight. There was for far too many of the adolescents a fundamental emptiness of purpose, a sense that they were not needed, not connected to adults, to tasks, to anything meaningful other than the raw and relentless pursuit of pleasure. And what empty pleasure seeking it was. Bereft of meaningful expectation, responsibilities, healthy options for recreation and entertainment, and with a notable absence of adults who were capable of being adults and active involved parents, these young people turned to the basest of impulses within and among themselves, with startling and pathetic results.

And as Beth Ross, director of Student Services for the Rockdale County Schools, suggests, "There are a lot of children who are running their own lives. Who really are testing the limits or don't know what the limits are. And they don't have the maturity. They don't have the experiences. They don't understand the consequences. I think there are many young people now who are very anxious about their lives and where they're headed and which way they are going."[27]

This disconnection is not happening just with students heading for trouble but also for their parents who watch in anguish as problems mount. Parent Beverly Lowry reports in her book *Crossed Over* about her lack of parenting skills.[28] Here's what she has to say about her son Peter, who was killed in an auto accident at age eighteen after a troubled, stormy youth. "You get so used to scaling down. Okay, so he won't go to college. Okay,

so maybe he will graduate from high school this year, so maybe never. So
he has a juvenile record, so he smokes dope. Okay, but—I used to think—
do I have to scale down so low as prison?"

As the *New York Times* book reviewer Francine Prose suggests, these
are a mother's anguished broodings as she tries, in retrospect, to trace a
happy little boy's transformation into an adolescent who somehow
stopped thinking of himself as a loving child. Through all of this runs an
acceptance of guilt and confusion, and an acknowledgment that these feelings may never end. "To this day I have no idea what I did for my two
boys that was constructive and useful and right and good, and what damaged them, none. It is a puzzle the whole way through, even now, when
my son Colin is grown with his own family. You never know anything, not
really. You never let yourself off the hook."[29]

Lowry's feelings of what went wrong can also be heard in the PBS
Frontline interview with Frank, the father of one of the teens involved in
the Rockdale crisis, as he talks about how his daughter Amy's life began
to change in middle school and the downward spiral that followed.[30]
Frank's words are sad and angry, and like his daughter, he feels a sense of
loss and questions what went wrong.

> And in those years it's where, you know, it was really just hard. I probably
> tried to maintain too much control and I couldn't. When her friends
> changed, that's when she started changing. You noticed a difference in her.
> She was not a happy child any more. It was like every night, you know, what
> can I do to go to my friends. It wasn't like, you know, every night I come
> home and get my homework and I go to bed and go to school and on the
> weekends I go to the movies and do what I can do. It was like every night
> goin' somewhere. She got involved with a group of friends and they smoke
> pot. That came to us when, well, she had gotten charged with it and they
> called me from jail that they had her there. And that's very devastating to a
> father who, you know, dotes on his children and their mother.

Frank also suggests a reason for Amy's downward spiral.

> She was very smart. She had good grades in school. And she won't tell you
> this. But I think she kind of dumbed herself down. What I mean is she didn't
> want to study in school. She didn't want to make the good grades because
> they would not accept her in the group. You got to be accepted somewhere.

Yeah. I just feel you're helpless. I know everybody probably has an idea in their mind what they want their kids to be and it certainly didn't involve anything like that. You get to the point where you see this happening and you are helpless. I'm not an educator and I don't know how. I didn't know how to get to her. I was full of advice. And to do it differently I would probably be more open to listen to what was going through their heads. 'Cause what's goin' through my mind was, "Look, how can we correct this, you know?" And certainly, then I'd give 'em advice, rather than listening to the problem. I would attack the immediate problem, not what was happening.

The work for educators is to find ways to intervene to help teens before acting out and addictive behaviors become a way of life, to find ways to connect with the twelve-year-old *Prozac Nation* girl and teen "cutters," the adolescents and parents of Rockdale County, *Thirteen*'s Tracy and parent Melanie, *Elephant*'s teens Alex, Eric, and John, and parents Mr. McFarland, Frank, and Beverly Lowry, before their problems spin out of control. We must learn how to quickly intervene when we see the Peter Lowrys, the Amys, and the Tracys of the world begin to change from happy little children into adolescents who stop thinking of themselves as loved children. We must, as the film *Elephant* advises, not turn a blind eye but rather look more closely at the problems no one at school or at home is noticing and teach the Melanies, Franks, Beverlys, and drunken Mr. McFarlands of the world how to listen, establish boundaries, and ask for help before it's too late.[31]

Too much time, energy, and resources of educators are now being wasted in punishment that can be transferred to develop intervention programs that work. We do have the data, the know-how, and the experience to include these programs in the school day without the need for new resources and personnel. As Resnick suggests:

Our research is showing us that parents, families, and adults outside of the family are fundamentally important to the healthy development of youth. Granted, many adolescents are very skillful at telling us, as adults, that we have become irrelevant in their lives. And *we* make the mistake of believing that! What is clear from the national studies of adolescent health and resilience is that caring and competent adults who recognize, value, and reward pro-social behavior in young people can have a profound effect on what adolescents value and believe about themselves and the world around them.[32]

And, as Resnick advises:

> The impact of connections in the lives of adolescents does not stop at the borders of the family. Indeed, we understand that adolescents who feel closely connected to their schools are adolescents who are emotionally healthier and far less likely to engage in risky behavior than their counterparts who feel no sense of community in their school, where school is not functioning as an arena of comfort. Without question it is the formation of friendship networks within the school that helps to provide that sense of community; along with the perception that teachers care, that teachers are fair, and that school is a place where one belongs.[33]

Sinclair and Ghory (1990) suggest that in forward-looking schools, principals, teachers, and parents bend over backward to create possibilities for productive connections. Students who are becoming marginalized receive a great deal of attention. Understanding how and why students become marginal provides a basis for action. Again, the first step begins with envisioning new ways to address children in trouble and admitting that what we do now isn't working for many students and parents, administrators, counselors, and teachers. As Rockdale School's educator Beth Ross puts it, "There are a larger and larger percentage of students looking at adults in the school to meet the needs they have."[34] We are all victims of an ineffective intervention system that is leaving us behind in our efforts to be a creditable source of help and guidance to these students. There are alternative models to follow.

However, in my experience in education reform efforts, resistance often preceded organizational change. Blame is sure to surface when it comes to making an honest assessment of how the intervention process is carried out in the schools. Blaming individual educators, groups, and issues for the breakdown of the intervention system quickly emerges when there is a call for change in the organization. It's part of the change process that must be faced early on and shown the door. Here are some of the arguments educators and parents will offer as to why the schools have failed to include more students and parents in the intervention process.

Some educators will say they have been pressured into focusing all their efforts on the business of schooling, such as raising test scores and moving students into the right classes and colleges. There is neither time nor energy to think change. Counselors will also be an early target with colleagues and parents, suggesting they should be doing more to help students resolve their problems and spend less time on testing, course selection, and college admissions. School nurses will also be targeted for not doing enough to identify and help students with health problems such as addiction, eating disorders, anxiety from school and family pressure, and poor nutrition, while in many schools nursing programs are being cut back due to budget woes. Teachers will come in for their share of the blame by those who say teachers should be more involved in helping students and not looking the other way or referring them on when trouble appears. And students themselves will be blamed for not being more open and helpful to their troubled peers. The same will be said of parents who seem unable to help their children and instead leave it to the school to solve their problems. And finally, school administrators will be blamed for not creating new ways of intervention and for staying instead with a system that is out of date.

But blaming doesn't help. In fact, we are kept in a state of denial and unchanging mode because it's easier to blame certain groups in the school and avoid any collective responsibility to make changes. It's easy to blame overextended counselors for not being there to assist each child. Counselors may have oversold their helping role but how can they offer schoolwide intervention to every student while at the same time being required to serve as quasi-administrators responsible for scheduling, college admissions, testing, and the like? The reality is that counselors are in a no-win situation, asked to do too much and in the end unable to deliver the needed intervention to students and parents. They represent a small group in the school and are an easy target.

School nurses, another isolated, small, and overextended group in the schools, are also an easy target. But like the counselors, they are unable to attend to the growing health and well-being problems coming into school each day. They, like the counselors, operate on a crisis schedule, dealing with the most critical situations, such as attempted suicide, drug overdose, or students experiencing physical, sexual, or emotional abuse. This is another no-win situation created by a flawed intervention system that cannot meet the expectations of the changing school environment. It is easy to blame untrained teachers for not being willing to help students they see headed for trouble. Because they have little training in helping and the advising process, we wrongly take teachers' resistance to the helping/advising role as a lack of commitment, of noncaring, even laziness. Harsh and, I believe, unfair labels.

It is easy to blame many students themselves who appear unwilling to help their troubled peers. But haven't we promoted the notion of achievement and doing whatever it takes to succeed and not asked students to be their brother's keeper? I believe that we, as educators, have failed to enlist them in a schoolwide caring process and to teach them simple helping techniques they could use in intervening in small ways to be helpful to their peers.

It's easy to blame parents for not being involved in helping guide neighborhood teens who are headed for trouble. The reality is that we haven't made overtures to parents to become involved as sources of help for students headed for trouble in our communities.

And, finally, it's easy to blame school administrators for not developing effective ways to leave no child behind. We need to keep in mind the reality that these educators are consumed each day, some overwhelmed, with maintaining order and putting out the countless fires that emerge each day with students, teachers, parents, and other staff.

Unfortunately some overworked administrators choose to accept this situation as the way it is. No, not intentionally. The fact is that many administrators become worn down physically and emotionally by the daily onslaught of students problems and the failure of the outdated intervention systems at their disposal to offer them, their staff, students, and parents some relief. It is a flawed system that is often hyped in the school district's public relations promotions as creating a safety net that "leaves no child behind" while, in reality, it does leave children behind. These administrators know that there is a growing need to address the personal and well-being needs of students and parents and find a new intervention model that can help them to redirect their and their schools' energies to win, rather than lose, the effort to leave no child behind, and to create a successful intervention model that allows them the time and energy to attend to other aspects of their leadership role that I have described in my book *An Administrator's Guide to Better Teacher Mentoring* (2002). These efforts include teacher mentoring, parent and community outreach, and positive contact with students from various groups in the school.[35]

The reality is that no one group in the school is to blame for the ineffective intervention system now in place. We inherited this system from the James B. Conant secondary school model developed in the 1950s that stressed the role of guidance counselors as the major source of student intervention and assigned students to counselors by grade and/or alphabet rather than by counseling skills such as individual and group counseling that might better serve to meet the personal and well-being needs of students and parents headed toward the margins.[36] That system has long outlived its usefulness and simply doesn't work in today's school world.

No matter which way we try to patch it up, it results in failure for all parties involved. We are all its victims. I would suggest that while problems and pressures created by high-stakes testing, school failure, and dropout and college admissions impact negatively on many students and add to their troubles, these are issues that we can help students and parents resolve if we begin to come to terms with the reality that these pressures are givens and they are not going to go away in the modern highly politicized schoolhouse. To do so we need new intervention systems to help guide our students and parents through the hazards posed by these pressures. In a sense we have created a trap for our students and parents and for ourselves as educators. We hear and respond to powerful voices that press us to focus only on the business of school but in the process we are failing to provide the necessary support to ensure that our students and parents are able to successfully navigate through these complicated parts of modern school life. We leave educators without the necessary tools and skills to offer effective intervention to their students.

We need to remember that many administrators, teachers, counselors, and school nurses went into the education field believing they could help students become all they could be—to help instill hope, foster dreams, and create opportunity in their students' worlds no matter what blows they may have suffered in their personal lives. They meant to be available to these students as they tried to navigate through the pitfalls of adolescent life. But as the business pressures of schools heat up, many caring educators find their value to the school system is increasingly related to increasing test scores. That's the reward.

However, in my observations, they are not being called upon, and trained, to talk with their students on a personal level, to notice the obvious symptoms of personal and well-being problems getting in the way of learning, and to listen and provide creditable advice, support, and sometimes referrals, to help students resolve problems before they explode into crisis and acting-out behaviors. In the process of revising our intervention system, a major emphasis must be placed on affirming, rewarding, and valuing educators for connecting with students on a personal level as well.

In my conversations with educators, many say they found their way into the classroom and principal's office because they themselves were helped by caring educators as teenagers. They found a caring adult who took time to listen, who advised, supported, and encouraged them to follow their dreams, and who served as advocates with parents and other teachers. These educators know firsthand that the key to student academic success and increased test scores begins with students being physically and mentally present in the class. And they know that students learn best in an inviting environment in which they are known, cared for, and listened to.

Therefore, as we begin the work of rethinking our intervention systems, a key component is the personal attention educators can offer students and parents. Our goal is to foster an organization in which achievement and high test scores matter and at the same time promote the notion that a human and caring connection of educators is a critical part of this process. It is a process in which counselors shift some of their helping responsibilities by training teachers, support staff, students, and parents to intervene on the front lines of the school; a process in which the health and well-being needs of students are served by school-based health clinics that utilize the medical resources of the community; a process in which school administrators recognize, value, and reward counselors, teachers, support staff, and student and parent leaders for connecting with students and parents on a personal level. This process requires administrators to use their position to sell, train, and empower the various members of the school community on the important role of being a helper, advisor, and source of support, to create a vision in which every member has a critical part to play in the intervention process.

Wager provides an excellent example of this creative process that must start with the principal's own thinking and interaction with staff and parents. As a new principal, Wager was faced with the conclusion that suspensions did not work to redirect students in a positive way—that teachers used the suspension process as a crutch. Observing the dependency on this failed system she reached the conclusion that neither "they [the teachers] nor I would be free to think creatively unless the pseudo-solution were abandoned. One year after my principalship began, I informed the staff that I would no longer suspend students and demanded that they propose alternative modes of discipline." In the exploration process to find alternatives to suspension Wager reports, "Our goal was to provide all teachers with the wisdom and self-restraint that had characterized the very best teachers all along." In the end, Wager, using her bully pulpit and prodding staff (she calls it "psychological brutality") to find alternatives, was successful.[37]

As she reports, "Teachers changed. Passivity and bitterness were replaced by enthusiastic participation. Students changed. They wished to be 'good citizens.' Parents changed as well. We had all underestimated the desire of parents for the education of their children. . . . Eventually, the disciplinary problems that had so tormented us shriveled to a negligible size. . . . Staff now spend more time on reform and renewal. Administrators are free to do more fruitful work of planning, communicating and coordinating." Wager concludes, "Educators must understand that the solution to their problems will not be found in sources external to themselves but rather, inside their own heads."[38]

I believe we have the resources at hand, beginning with Wager's advice that it is "inside our own heads, to successfully intervene to help each child resolve the personal and well-being issues that are serving as barriers to their successful learning."[39] Yes, we know what is not working, but we need greater awareness of our dependency on these failed solutions. What is required is a reconfiguration of the helping groups and resources in the school: pupil personnel workers that include counselors, school psychologist, social worker, and student assistance counselors; teachers; administrators, school nurses; support staff; students; parents and community counseling and health agencies.

How do we begin to develop a new model of intervention that calls upon the helping resources of every member of the school community, a model in which every professional, support staff member, student, and parent serves as his or her brother's keeper? Authors Sinclair and Ghory (1990) suggest that the term at risk may work against what we hope to accomplish with the sizable portion of young people who are headed for trouble in school. Embedded in each description of a problem is an implied intervention approach.

The "at risk" language focuses on a population of students considered unlikely to succeed. The term at risk tends to isolate and stereotype these youngsters. Too often, one implication of such labeling is for educators and politicians to cluster these students in special groups for intensive treatment of their academic and social ills. The terminology easily lends itself to an overemphasis on identifying those students considered at risk, with the accompanying fascination with the quantification of variables that will predict or sort out who fits the at-risk label. The first and main problem becomes determining who these students are, rather than creating conditions that correct these disabilities. The identification-quantification mentality sometimes may lead to fallacious reasoning that increased test scores are evidence that the school is making progress with disconnected kids.

However, and more to my point that we need many open doors through which students headed for trouble can walk for help, Sinclair and Ghory (1990) suggest that it is sobering to realize that anyone is at risk of becoming at least temporarily disconnected from full and productive involvement in classrooms and school. Anyone can be quickly knocked out of a pattern of productivity and go unattended at school for long periods. Unfortunately these problems do not go away. They fester and can reach a boiling point in the late teen years or in early adult life. Time is not always a healer. As a result of a lack of intervention, problems can become more complicated and serious.

Sinclair and Ghory (1990) wisely urge educators to use the term "marginal" to move away from the potentially negative and divisive connotations connected with most labels used to describe young people who have difficult relations with school. Use of the term marginal to explain learning shifts the perspective away from deeply seated problems rooted in the individual to problematic relationships between individuals and the school environment.

Rather, the crucial issue is the extent to which the school environment can respond productively to the variations among students. When students are seen moving to the margins of a classroom or school, it is necessary to question what conditions in the school–student relationship are not working. Rather than providing a means to separate individuals and their behaviors neatly into two categories—normal and at risk—the marginal perspective highlights the fact that any individual's action is always relative and changeable, a matter of degree. The degree of school marginality depends not only on the characteristics of the student actor or action but even more on the ways in which the person or his or her behavior is interpreted and treated by educators.

Problematic behaviors are not an individual's total personality and behavior repertoire. In part, they are response to how a person is being treated. Marginal learners can change even deep-seated, unproductive habits, just as constructive adjustments can be made in relatively static educational environments. There is no single point at which an individual becomes marginal or nonmarginal once and for all. It is necessary, therefore, to understand the path to becoming marginal and the ways in which educators can collaborate to reintegrate individuals with an improved and responsive school environment.

A major theme in this book, then, is about how to create a number of open doors in the school that students and parents in need of help and support with learning, personal, and well-being problems can walk through with ease and support and in the process foster an organization that promotes, and sells, the notion that we are here for "all" our students in time of need. The National Association of Secondary Schools 2004 report, *Executive Summary of Breaking Ranks 11: Strategies for Leading High School Reform*, suggests that educator leaders are looking for concrete ways to respond to the growing personal and well-being problems of students that can negatively impact on their learning and development.[40] The report's recommendations provide direction for high school principals across the country in making schools more student centered via personalized programs, support services, and intellectual rigor. Here are some of the report's recommendations:

1. The principal will provide leadership in the high school community by building and maintaining a vision, direction, and focus on student learning.
2. The school will provide every student with meaningful adult relationships that can best support every student.
3. The aspirations, strengths, and weaknesses of each student should be known by at least one faculty member or other member of the staff,

and the staff members should use this information to help the student become successful in all classes and activities.

4. The school should implement a comprehensive advisory program that ensures that each student has frequent and meaningful opportunities to plan and assess his or her academic and social progress with a faculty member. Every student then will have a personal adult advocate to help him or her to personalize the educational experience.

5. Teachers will convey a sense of caring to their students so that students feel that their teachers share a stake in their learning.

6. The high school will engage students' families as partners in the students' education. The school leadership team will provide ways to successfully interact with hard-to-reach parents with activities such as home visits, Saturday meetings, and meetings outside of regular business hours.

7. High schools, in conjunction with agencies in the community, will help coordinate the delivery of physical and mental health and social services to youth.

These are important and valuable recommendations. It is my hope that this book provides a road map for busy school administrators, pupil personnel workers such as counselors and school psychologists, teacher leaders, and parent advocates on how to design more personalized support services in the schools that *Breaking Ranks 11* calls for. As the *Breaking Ranks 11* report suggests, the idea for comprehensive change may not begin in the principal's office, but it most assuredly can end either through incomplete planning, failure to involve others, neglect, or failure to create conditions that allow a new order of things to emerge in the high school. Creating those conditions is often the first challenge, and sometimes it must start within the principal's own thinking and interactions with people.

The remaining chapters in the book serve as a guide for principals on how they can proceed to create a vision of high school student support services that is dramatically different from past models and ready and set to respond to students and parents in today's and tomorrow's school world. In a sense this book is the next step in my efforts to help principals and teachers leaders create a schoolwide intervention system that utilizes the helping resources of each member of the school community.

My book *An Administrator's Guide to Better Teacher Mentoring* (2002) set out a plan on how to develop effective teacher mentoring practices. I followed this book with *An Educator's Guide to Understanding the Personal Side of Students' Lives*, a guide for administrators on how to develop effective teacher advising programs. This book focuses in on helping administrators develop more effective ways to gather data about students heading toward the margins, redesigning and decentralizing guidance intervention programs, and providing training for students, support staff, and parents on how they can serve as reliable sources of help and referral for students and parents when trouble emerges. By including every member of the school community and expecting him or her to serve as reliable sources of help, this process can serve to reform schools and act on many of the recommendations of the NASSP *Breaking Ranks 11* report for more student-centered schools, schools in which every community member learns not to turn a blind eye. This book invites them to look closely at the problems of school and home and take notice of the small things in the lives of students and their parents that can drain a heart of feeling.

Sinclair and Ghory (1990) suggest that students at the margins are a crucial problem that must be addressed in the next phase of education reform. By starting with the problems of marginal students, it may be possible to move in a deliberate manner to redefine roles and responsibilities that educators have toward students.

In the end, this effort is about creating what researchers Simmons and Blyth (1987) call "arenas of comfort" for students and, I would suggest, for parents. Their research suggests that if change comes too suddenly, that is, if there is too much discontinuity with prior experience, or if change is too early given the children's cognitive and emotional states, or if it occurs in too many areas of life at once, then presumably individuals will experience great discomfort. They will experience discomfort with self and discomfort with the world. Such children will not feel at one with themselves nor at home in the social environment.

Individuals should do better both in terms of self-esteem and behavioral coping if there is some area of comfort in their lives. The need for an arena of comfort would explain why more gradual changes upon entry to adolescence appear beneficial, as do fewer simultaneous changes. If the individual is comfortable in some environments, life arenas, and role relationships, then discomfort in another arena can be tolerated and mastered.

It is understandable that youngsters are less able to cope if at one and the same time they are uncomfortable with their bodies, due to physical changes; with their family, due to changes in family constellation; with home, because of a move; with school, due to great discontinuity in the nature of the school environment; and with peers because of the new importance of the opposite sex relationships and because of disruption of prior peer networks in a new school and changes in peer expectations and peer evaluation criteria. Simmons and Blyth (1987) conclude that there needs to be some arena of life or some set of role relationships with which the individual can feel relaxed and comfortable, to which he or she can withdraw and become reinvigorated—reinvigorated so that the child learns how to cope with large-scale organizational environments with all their opportunities as well as their impersonality.

I believe we need to embrace Simmons and Blyth's (1987) recommendations and envision a new kind of intervention model that provides a number of arenas of comfort and role relationships in our schools that can offer students and parents the opportunity to feel safe, comfortable, and accepted and to learn new skills to cope with the personal and well-being problems that are getting in the way of their dreams, gifts, and hopes. This is not to say that arenas of comfort will be a cure-all for every acting-out student. Some students will continue to be difficult and may need help outside the school setting. But by acting early on to help every child as they head toward trouble, I believe we can dramatically reduce the number of adolescents who become unmanageable and alienated in our secondary schools.

Chapter 2, "Paying Attention to Students Headed toward the Margins," focuses on how principals can begin this effort by creating a comprehensive program to gather and centralize data about students headed toward the margins and in the process extend the label of "who" is offered intervention in the school. Chapter 3, "Creating an Effective Student Intervention System," focuses on how principals can create a new decentralized intervention model that can quickly respond to marginal students. The last chapter of the book, "How a Crisis Spurred an Intervention System at One High School," focuses on a case study of how a decentralized intervention model emerged in one high school.

NOTES

1. William L. Fibkins, *An Educator's Guide to Understanding the Personal Side of Student's Lives* (Lanham, Md.: Scarecrow Press, 2003), 3.

2. Barbara Ries Wager, "No More Suspensions: Creating a Shared Ethical Culture," *Educational Leadership 50*(4) (December 1992–January 1993): 34–37.

3. William Blythe, "All the Children Are above Average," *New York Times*, March 14, 2004, pp. 6, 7.

4. "Comprehensive Bill to Truly Leave No Child Behind," Unveiling of Dodd-Miller Act, 2003; www.cdfactioncouncil.org/ALNCB_reintroduction_PR.html (accessed 6 March 2004).

5. Centers for Disease Control and Prevention (2003), *Stories from the Field: Lessons Learned about Building Coordinated School Health Programs* (Atlanta: Centers for Disease Control and Prevention, 2003), xxi, 1–3.

6. David M. Herszenhorn, "Broad Overhaul in New York City to Replace Many Middle Schools." *New York Times*, 3 March 2004, pp. 1, 6 (B).

7. Laura Pappano, "In ADHD Debate, No Right Answers," Boston.com, 2004; www.boston.com/news/education/k_12/articles/2004/03/07/in_adhed_debate-no_right_answer (accessed 8 March 2004).

8. Lisa N. Staresina, "Student Mobility," *Education Week 2003*; www.edweek.org/context/topics/issuepage.cfm>id+82 (accessed 14 January 2004).

9. Roberta G. Simmons, and Dale A. Blyth, *Moving into Adolescence: The Impact of Puberty Changes and School Context* (New York: Aldine De Gruyter, 1987), xii, 304, 351–352.

10. Brigid McMenamin, "Turning to Tutors Instead of Schools," *New York Times*, 26 October 2003, p. 5 (BU).

11. Bill Pennington, "As Sports Teams Conflict, Some Parents Rebel," *New York Times*, 12 November 2003, pp. 1, 7 (D).

12. Margaret Talbot, "Play Date with Destiny," *New York Times Magazine*, 21 September 2003, pp. 31–35, 52, 64, 82–83 (6).

13. Darcy Frey, "Betrayed by the Game," *New York Times Magazine*, 15 February 2004, pp. 14, 16, 18–19 (6).

14. Ylan Q. Mui, "Scandals Stun Howard County in Academic Year Gone Sour," washingtonpost.com, 2004; www.washingtonpost.com/ac2/wp-dyn/A24026-2004Febi?language=printer (accessed 2 June 2004).

15. Timothy Egan, "Body Conscious Boys Adopt Athletes' Taste for Steroids," *New York Times*, 22 November 2002, pp. 1, 24 (A).

16. Erica Goode, "Stronger Warning Is Urged on Antidepressants for Teenagers," *New York Times*, 3 February 2004, p. 12 (A).

17. Thomas Fowler-Finn, "Profile," in *Adolescents at School: Perspectives on Youth, Identity, and Education*, ed. Michael Sadowski (Boston: Harvard Education Press, 2003), 5, 31–34.

18. Roger Ebert, "The Perfect Score," *Chicago Sun-Times* 2004; www.sun times.com/cgi-bin/print.cgi (accessed 2 August 2004).

19. Cynthia Lightfoot, *The Culture of Adolescent Risk-Taking* (New York: The Guilford Press, 1997), 15.

20. National Center for Education Statistics (NCES), "Principals' Perception of Discipline Issues in Their Schools," NCES 1996–1997; www.nces.edgov/ pubs98/violence/98030007.html (accessed 3 August 2002).

21. Robert L. Sinclair, and Ward J. Ghory, "Last Things First: Realizing Equality by Improving Conditions for Marginal Students," in *Access to Knowledge: An Agenda for Our Nation's Schools*, eds. John I. Goodlad and Pamela Keating (New York: College Entrance Board, 1990), 129–130, 132–133, 137.

22. Hollywood.com, "Prozac Nation," Hollywood.com 2004; http://hollywood .com/movies/detail/movies/376226 (accessed 28 July 2004).

23. Michelle Galley, "Student Self-Harm: Silent School Crisis," *Education Week* 2003; www.edweek.org/ew/ewstory.cfm?Slug=14cutters.h23 (accessed 14 January 2004).

24. Elvis Mitchell, "Trading Barbie for Drugs, Sex, and Halter Tops," *New York Times*, 20 August 2003, pp. 1, 5 (E).

25. Elvis Mitchell, "'Normal' High School on the Verge," *New York Times*, 10 October 2003, pp. 1, 24 (E).

26. Michael D. Resnick, "Adrift in America: The Lost Children of Rockdale County," PBS *Frontline* Interview 2003; www.pbs.org/wgbh/pages/frontline/shows/ georgia/isolated/resnick.html (accessed 28 January 2004).

27. Beth Ross, "The Lost Children of Rockdale County," PBS *Frontline* Interview 2003; www.pbs.org.wgbh/pages/frontline/shows/georgia/interviews/beth .html (accessed 11 March 2004).

28. Francine Prose, "Close to Home," *New York Times*, 23 August 1992, pp. 1, 21–22 (7).

29. Prose, "Close to Home."

30. Frank, "The Lost Children of Rockdale County," PBS *Frontline* Interview 2003; www.pbs.org/wgbh/pages/frontline/shows/georgia/interviews/frank.html (accessed 13 March 2004).

31. Peter Travers, "Elephant," rollingstone.com 2003; www.rollingstone.com/ reviews/movie/review.asp?mid=2047649 (accessed 16 March 2004).

32. Resnick, "Adrift in America."

33. Resnick, "Adrift in America."

34. Ross, "The Lost Children of Rockdale County."

35. William L. Fibkins, *An Administrator's Guide to Better Teacher Mentoring* (Lanham, Md.: Scarecrow Press, 2002).

36. James B. Conant, *The American High School Today* (New York: McGraw-Hill, 1959), 44, 78, 81, 93–94, 96.

37. Wager, "No More Suspensions: Creating a Shared Ethical Culture."

38. Wager, "No More Suspensions: Creating a Shared Ethical Culture."

39. Wager, "No More Suspensions: Creating a Shared Ethical Culture."

40. National Association of Secondary School Principals (NASSP), *Executive Summary of Breaking Ranks 11: Strategies for Leading High School Reform* (Reston, Va.: NASSP, 2004), 1–6.

2

Paying Attention to Students Headed toward the Margins

Data about students headed toward the margins of school life abounds in the school. Educators who pay close attention to this data are ready and set to help students headed toward the margins of school life. This information can be found in the formal accounting records such as daily attendance, tardiness, class cutting, suspensions, expulsions, number of dropouts, academic success and failure, retentions, health records and visits to the nurse's office, teacher observations, frequency of parent visits to school and parent–teacher meetings, referrals to counseling, participation or lack of participation in extracurricular activities, and abuse of tobacco, alcohol, and drugs.

Information about students headed for trouble can also be identified in informal contacts such as conversations between students and peers; from support staff, such as lunchroom monitors and secretaries; observations from homeroom and classroom teachers; and from school bus drivers, custodial staff, extracurricular club leaders, coaches, school nurses, concerned neighborhood parents, community recreation, and church outreach workers. Certain settings in the school in which student conversations flow freely, such as in lunchrooms, at dances and athletic events, in the hallways between classes, at hangout areas for student smokers and class cutters, and in detention rooms, are prime sources of this informal information, as are community recreation and teen centers.

However, in most schools this formal data is scattered in many different places in the school, such as with the assistant principal or in the counselor and nurse's offices, and often is not collected in a central data system, analyzed and ready to use as a basis to intervene to help students. For example, the counseling office may store data on test results, applications to colleges, and grades. The assistant principal's office may store data on attendance, truancy, class cutting, and suspensions, with a special emphasis on monitoring the "usual suspects," also known as the at-risk group. The nurse's office, while having a wealth of information about the number of student visits, the health issue involved, and parent contacts, often lacks computer access.

In many schools there is no centralized database that includes the variety of information that is readily available on each student. When information is collected, it is often used to deflect blame and demonstrate that the school is succeeding, such as reducing the number of dropouts or increasing the number of students heading toward select colleges and universities. Data then is often viewed as a public relations tool to answer critics and promote successes.

The huge amount of information garnered from the observations of administrators, teachers, counselors, social workers, school psychologists, support staff, peers, and community outreach workers is also often scattered or unused in gathering data needed for an effective intervention system. Some teachers will seek out a counselor, a school nurse, or an assistant principal when they listen to a student conversation about an imminent crisis, such as a possible suicide attempt. However, many professional staff, support staff, custodial staff, students, and concerned parents do not see it as their role or their job to share their concern about a student headed for trouble. They think that because they are not trained counselors, their observations and input are not valuable.

And more important, there are few open doors in the school that they can easily walk through and share their data and their concern. The designated "open door" in the school—the counseling, nurse's, and assistant principal's offices—are busy places, not arenas of comfort as Roberta G. Simmons and Dale A. Blyth suggest.[1] Much of the helpful data gathered on the front lines of the school does not find its way into the database for students. Rather, it sits in the minds of professional and support staff, peers and concerned parents, often raising conflicting feelings about why they are not acting to do something to help this student and in some cases fearing that if something happens to this student it will be their fault.

As Warren Torgerson argues, even though we have a wealth of observables, there is a serious lack of important connections.[2] Researcher Kenneth A. Sirotnik is right on target when he suggests that given the resources ordinarily available at the building level, districts must take an active role in supporting, nurturing, and sustaining the collection of information in schools.[3] Statistical software and programming capability must be supported in order to select and merge files, cases, and variables and conduct the appropriate analysis. As Sirotnik suggests, creative use of resources and talents is the ticket here. It is not difficult to imagine districts setting schools up with their own capacity for doing the basic analyses on computers.

Therefore, the first step for administrators in designing a new intervention program is to focus on ways to collect and use this data as an important tool in an ongoing effort to understand and monitor which students are drifting into personal, academic, and well-being problems; educate professional and support staff, peers, and concerned parents that any student in the school is capable of heading toward the margins; create a number of open doors that invite professional and support staff, peers, parents, and community health and social service professionals to share a concern about a student headed for trouble; and receive needed advice, guidance, and support. In a sense, this first step is both a leadership and a teaching role. We must use the principal's bully pulpit to enlist every member of the school community as helping resources. In a helping community, members serve as their brothers' keepers, take notice when problems emerge and act to intervene, not look the other way and hope someone else will act for them.

In addition to the formal and informal data available, the database should also include recommendations from *Breaking Ranks 11* that schools need to identify the aspirations, strengths, and weaknesses of each student; identify professional staff members who facilitate interactions with hard-to-reach parents; and, when available, a community contact involved in the delivery of physical and mental health and social services to a student or group of students.[4] In other words, focus on the dreams and needs that each student brings into the school community and those adults in the school and community who are responsible for knowing and interacting with this student and are accountable for this important data.

What we need to be about is developing access to credible data in order to generate more interest and commitment by professional and support staff, peers, parents, and community members to the well-being of every child. This database should have three major components. First, a formal component that contains specific up-to-date information on each student, such as strengths, achievement, and aspirations, as well as academic and well-being areas that need support. Second, an informal component that culls information about each student from observations of administrators, teachers, counselors, concerned students, parents, and outreach resources in the community. Third, an organization in the school, such as a Kids in Need Committee, that serves as a funnel for this data and develops an intervention plan when a student is observed heading for trouble and the margins of school life.

In terms of a formal database in the schools, I am advocating for the creation of a student well-being profile (SWP), a database that enables educators to quickly assess and monitor the academic strengths and level of well-being of each student and those areas that need improvement. In a sense the SWP that I envision is similar to a scouting report used to identify the strengths and skills of athletes and those areas that need improvement and more work. For example, in scouting reports on baseball pitchers, such variables as speed, variety of pitches, win and loss record, earned run average, bases on balls awarded, strikeouts, runs given up, and innings pitched are regularly assessed and when the data suggests trouble, such as too many bases on balls, intervention is quickly provided. Every effort is made to not allow players to drift and remain stuck with bad habits that inevitably lead to failure. The SWP I am arguing for, then, is a way of looking at each student through a positive lens, assessing where we need to intervene and help those students to succeed and improve the quality of their school lives.

As author Ann Hulbert suggests, "what gets measured gets done."[5] I believe the development of computer technology in our secondary schools now creates the opportunity to develop an SWP in every secondary school. School administrators should be able to have an SWP for each student at their disposal that can be easily accessed through their computer. They should be able to use this file to extract trends and problem areas that are impacting negatively on students and set the stage for quick intervention.

For example, researchers Margaret C. Wang, Maynard C. Reynolds, and Herbert J. Walberg recommend stepping up research on marginal students to provide a growing knowledge base and credible evaluation system.[6] They suggest that there are promising practices to reduce suspension rates. They warn that where there are no data, it is too easy to conclude there are no problems or to describe problems with vague generalities. Research should address strengths, resilience, and similar positive factors, as well as limitations and deficiencies.

In summary, there are five important and related first steps that administrators must take in designing a student well-being profile and effective intervention system:

1. Develop a centralized database that includes formal data as well as the aspirations, strengths, and weaknesses of each student; the name of their personal adult advocate, when appropriate; the names of professional staff responsible for contact with hard-to-reach parents; and the names of community physical and mental health and social services professionals involved with the student. Here is a list of some of the specific data that should be available for each student (this is a beginning list; educators may wish to add data):
   - Name
   - Address
   - Telephone number
   - Date of birth
   - Name of parent(s) or guardian(s)
   - Marital status of parent(s) or guardian(s)
   - Name of employer of parent(s) or guardian(s)
   - Names and ages of siblings
   - Sex
   - Race/ethnicity
   - Name of personal adult advocate in school
   - Name of counselor
   - Name of homeroom teacher
   - Name of physician
   - Health coverage
   - Aspirations
   - Strengths
   - Weaknesses/areas that need attention
   - Remediation needed
   - Physical handicapping conditions

- Emotional handicapping conditions
- Newcomer to school
- Dates of parent/guardian contacts
- Reasons for parent/guardian contacts
- Outcome of parent/guardian contacts
- Parent/guardian no-show for school contacts
- Grades
- Grade point average
- Previous retentions
- Test scores
- Special achievements and honors
- Involvement in extracurricular activities
- Attendance
- Tardiness to school
- Tardiness to class
- Class cuts
- Detentions
- Suspensions
- Expulsions
- Summer school attendance
- Dates of visits to nurse's office
- Reasons for visits to nurse's office
- Outcome of visits to nurse's office
- Dates of visits to counselor's office
- Reasons for visits to counselor's office
- Outcome of visits to counselor's office
- Referrals to Child Study Team
- Referrals to school psychologist
- Referrals to social worker
- Referrals to community mental health agencies
- Referrals to community health agencies
- Referrals for rehabilitation

2. Foster and promote the expectation that the informal observations about students by professional and support staff, peers, and concerned parents are important and necessary contributions to the process of creating a database in developing a schoolwide intervention program.

3. Foster and promote the expectation that the resources, observations, and feedback of community health and social service groups are important and necessary contributions to creating a database in developing a school–community intervention network.

4. Foster and promote the expectation that many open doors need to be created in the school through which concerned professional and support staff, peers, neighborhood parents, and community resources can walk to share their concerns about students and in the process expect to receive credible advice and guidance on how to proceed to be an ongoing source of help and support for students. These must be easily accessible venues in the school that serve the purpose of collecting data about students and parents who may need intervention.

   One example of the open doors I am talking about, where students' stories and troubles become known, is the creating of a principal-led agency in the school, such as the Kids in Need Committee, which serves as a resource to receive the formal and informal data about students and is ready and set to develop an intervention plan when students are identified as heading toward the margins. The Kids in Need Committee should be composed of the principal and leaders from the teaching staff, school psychologist, social worker, counseling staff, and community resource person. They should meet on a weekly basis; serve as a contact for concerned educators, support staff, and community resources; provide an open invitation for these individuals to present their concerns at weekly meetings; and provide release time for them so they can make their concerns known.

5. Foster and create the expectation that many open doors need to be created in the school through which students and parents can walk to get help in resolving personal, academic, and well-being problems. As Frank DeAngelis, principal of Columbine High School, reported on the fifth anniversary of the Columbine shootings, "Columbine served as a wake-up call for the nation. The biggest thing that needs to be done nationwide is making sure that kids have a place to go to express themselves and seek help."[7] This is sound advice from an educator who knows the cost of creating a first-rate academic school organization but not an organization prepared to intervene to address the emotional well-being of some students headed toward the margins of school life.

As Margaret A. McKenna, president of Lesley University says about Columbine, "Five years ago automatic weapons fire echoed through the halls of Columbine High School, shattering not only lives but the complacency of that high-achieving suburban school."[8] McKenna says that as a result of the shootings there was widespread acknowledgment that teachers and administrators needed to find ways to know kids better and create real communities in the school. I believe one workable model of providing an open door for concerned students and parents is the creation of a student assistance counselor in the school, a member of the counseling staff whose major focus is offering individual and group counseling for students and parents headed toward the margins, guidance and support for teachers and administrators, and referral to community counseling, rehabilitation, and health agencies. The creation of such a role clearly identifies a "go to" person in the school when a peer or parent has a concern about a student's behavior or the troubled student himself or herself decides to seek help.

I believe this effort by principals to create, foster, and promote a new kind of intervention system can offer help and support to students from every group in the school who are headed toward the margins. Part of this process calls on principals to clearly lay out a picture of the academic, emotional, and well-being costs that students and their parents encounter as they head toward the margins of school life. They must point out that students headed toward the margins have emotional costs for professional and support staff, peers, and neighborhood parents who observe a student in trouble but do not know how to intervene. Costs for students and parents come in many forms.

For some students changes in their lives come much too quickly. A barrage of misfortunes arrives with no let up. An adolescent, once a happy child, is unprepared for the adult problems and issues he or she faces. Children become adults overnight, sometimes forced to take care of siblings while a single parent works or to live with an abusive relative while the parents "get their lives together." A divorce, a move to a new home and school, a death or serious illness of a parent, or a move to a larger school can overwhelm teenagers. Sometimes there are multiple changes, all arriving at once and serving to assault the health and well-being of students trying to get a handle on the fast pace of change. For other students the cost is more serious and can result in death from a suicide or accident. Costs for professional and support staff, peers, and concerned parents come from noticing a student struggling but who, in the end, as the educators in Gus Van Sant's film *Elephant*, turn a blind eye.[9]

Therefore, it is critical that administrators use their opportunities to educate members of the school community about the costs for students and parents headed toward the margins and costs for professional and support staff, neighborhood parents, and community members when they turn a blind eye. Here are some examples of costs to students and their parents that might have been avoided if their school had an effective intervention system in place that included a personal adult advocate who knew the student, interacted with him or her on a regular basis, communicated with and advised the student's parent or guardian, and served as an advocate for the student with teachers and administrators, someone who noticed, as the review of *Elephant* suggests, "the small things that can drain a heart of feeling." These are examples administrators can use to motivate professional and support staff, students, parents, and community groups to shift from the role of observers on the sidelines to a proactive helping role, a role that focuses on leaving no child behind, even the standard-bearers who may find themselves heading for trouble.

THE CASE OF ROB PACE

The case of Rob Pace vividly portrays what can happen to students when they are suddenly thrust toward the margins of life and have no open door, arena of comfort, or personal adult advocate. Rob had loving and accepting parents, Robert and Karen. But they had no idea that their son was in serious conflict. As reported by Ryan Cormier, Rob was an eighteen-year-old senior at Riverhead High School on Long Island, New York, who after being arrested on drug possession charges during a school trip to Six Flags Great Adventure amusement park in New Jersey in April 2000 was forbidden by school officials to return home on the school bus.[10] After the arrest, Pace was released by police and then made his way, alone, to Manhattan and boarded a Long Island Railroad train in Penn Station and committed suicide later that night.

Pace, a member of the National Honor Society, wrote a note saying he was sorry for "letting anyone . . . down" before he jumped between the cars of a moving train near Bethpage, New York. Riverhead school officials ordered the bus to leave without him. He was left in New Jersey on April 14, 2000, alone, distraught, and suicidal.

The events in this tragic episode are worth reviewing. Cormier reports it was April 14 when trouble started as Pace, along with eighty classmates and eight chaperones, entered the New Jersey amusement park. Pace's keys set off the metal detector and he was searched by park security as the school chaperones walked on, unaware he had been stopped. Six Flags Great Adventure security found a small amount of cocaine, four ecstasy pills, and two and a half marijuana cigarettes in Rob's backpack, and he was immediately arrested by Jackson, New Jersey, police.

Because he was eighteen, police allowed Pace to leave after paying station house bail once he was processed and released. He was charged with misdemeanor drug possession.

While nobody knows for sure how he got back to New York, it is known that he was on the 9:05 Long Island Rail Road train that left from Penn Station. While on the train, he wrote a suicide letter on the back of his physics assignment, apologizing to his parents and sister for disappointing them, his parents say. "I'm so sorry," he wrote. "I never wanted it to end like this, but unfortunately I put myself here." He signed the note, "Love forever, Rob." Police told Pace's mother, Karen, that a woman on the train watched as he placed the note on top of his backpack, left the pack, and walked away, never coming back. After the woman told the conductor someone had left a bag in the train, it was discovered that Pace had jumped between the cars of the moving train. "He had eleven hours to sit there alone, surrounded by strangers, to badger himself about this," said Pace's father, Robert, of the time between the arrest and his son's suicide. "It blew his life away," Karen Pace said, adding that she knew of no other pressing problems in his life.

Two weeks after Pace's suicide, the family received the transcripts of conversations between the police and school authorities from April 14. On the tapes, Joseph Ogeka, then the assistant principal of Riverhead High School, told the arresting officer that Pace was not going to be allowed on the school bus. "I don't want him going back on the bus with our kids," he said. "He's eighteen, he can do what he wants."

There were many lost opportunities to help Rob. His suicide probably could have been avoided if the response by Riverhead school officials had demonstrated concern for him. Instead, the school officials appear to have used the event to send a message to Rob, the other students on the field trip, the chaperones, and the entire Riverhead school community that there is zero tolerance for such behavior. They suggested, by denying him a safe return on the bus, that Rob was no longer a member of the school community. He broke the rules. We are no longer responsible for him, even if he is an honor student and standard-bearer. We're cutting him loose. He's off the bus. We don't want him contaminating the other students.

And Rob's suicide probably could have been avoided if just one chaperone had come forward to challenge the decision to leave Rob on his own and offered to stay by his side. But it appears that everyone in the end turned a blind eye to Rob's dilemma. All the students, except Rob, were seated on the bus and accounted for. Imagine how those students felt leaving their friend behind to fend for himself. Imagine their thoughts on what would happen to them if some day down the road they too broke the rules. Who would be there for them? Imagine the thoughts of the chaperones, who were surely torn about the decision to leave Rob on his own far from home, but at the same time being good soldiers and following orders. Imagine their thoughts on what might happen to them if some day down the road they, too, broke the rules. Who would be there for them? And imagine the thoughts of Riverhead school officials like principal Joseph Ogeka. He too is probably torn by his decision to leave Rob on his own. "He's eighteen, he can do what he wants." He probably wishes he had that decision to make over.

It appears that there was plenty to blame and find fault with. The pillars of a healthy school community—teaching by example, leaving no child behind, teaching students to be their brother's keeper, and as the *Breaking Ranks 11* report recommends, "the high school community will advocate and model a set of core values essential in a democratic society"—appeared absent. However, as in many stories of loss, schools need to provide ways for healing and to use the event to restructure their intervention and caring efforts so the adults responsible for the care of students take notice and act. For example, what kinds of support, open doors for help, were available to the students and chaperones on the field trip, the Riverhead High School students, faculty, and parents, and for Joseph Ogeka himself as they searched to make sense out of this loss?

Perhaps one positive outcome will be for Riverhead High School and other high schools to be mindful that many kinds of students, not just the ones labeled as at risk, may need intervention as they head toward the margins. Schools need to make sure that their intervention antenna has a wide focus and that every child has the opportunity for a successful passage to adulthood with the help of caring teachers, peers, families, and community members. Rob Pace wasn't an at-risk kid who cut class, did poorly in school, or stirred up trouble. He was a standard-bearer, was a member of the National Honor Society, and had been accepted at Quinnipiac College. Yet he was still a kid finding his way and making mistakes in the process, even though he was eighteen.

The spring before graduation is often a time for high school seniors to be less cautious. Rob brought drugs on a field trip, not a smart move. But as his mother said, she knew of no other pressing problems in his life. But on April 14 he needed help and intervention. His absence from the group at the amusement park needed to be noticed. He had eleven hours to spend on his own. We need to imagine what it was like for him, thinking about how he was going to face his parents and classmates. We also need to retrace the steps in this event and identify the many opportunities that were available to act toward the Rob Paces of this world so this type of event is not repeated.

Rob's suicide did result in a major change. According to reporter Joshi Pradnya, New York State Governor George Pataki signed a law sponsored by New York State Assemblywoman Patricia Acampora on July 13, 2001, that requires school districts either to bring back students on class trips or assign a chaperone to any student left behind. Acampora says, "You put your child in someone's hands and you hope that they do the right thing."[11]

MEPHAM HIGH SCHOOL HAZING

In some school groups, students headed toward the margins choose to remain silent and not ask for help. These students are not on the list of at-risk students, as one might expect. They are athletes trying to win a spot on the team's roster. And part of the cost of winning a spot on the team sometimes involves participating in rites of passage such as hazing. In a real sense these young athletes, ninth and tenth grade students, are victims of long-held hazing practices that are well known but often ignored in the school community. Students, staff, parents, and administrators look the other way. But sometimes these hazing practices get out of hand and athletes become victims of abuse. These victims are often bullied into silence, forced to keep the abuse to themselves, hidden from adult advocates and parents who could offer help and support. This is what happened at Mepham High School, located in Nassau County on Long Island, New York, in 2003 and probably years preceding the uncovering of the abuse.

"Schooled in Overlooking Trouble" is the headline in reporter Paul Vitello's commentary on a Wayne County, Pennsylvania, grand jury report on hazing carried out by older players both at a football camp held in the summer of 2003 in Pennsylvania and at Mepham High School.[12] The hazing left three young players tortured, sodomized, and humiliated during the team's 2003 preseason training camp in the Pocono township of Preston Park in August 2003. It also left three player perpetrators tried and convicted in juvenile court, the football season canceled, the community torn apart. And as Vitello reports, it left the name of Mepham tied in the public mind for the foreseeable future to the image of thugs in Mepham jerseys forcing broomsticks into the bodies of terrified younger players while many of their teammates stood around laughing. The grand jury reported, "These assaults appear to have grown out of a custom or history of hazing both at the football camp and at Mepham High School itself," and suggested that someone in charge, at some point over the years, should have learned of these attacks by older players, the team leaders, against younger, vulnerable newcomers. But as Vitello reports, the five Mepham coaches who chaperoned the team and school administrators of the Bellmore-Merrick school district insist they never heard of such a thing.

Upon closer examination, the so-called team leaders and perpetrators of the attacks were troubled students headed toward the margins of school life. Some educators and parents who turned a blind eye to their abusive behaviors and gave them a green light to continue these practices knew their acting-out and abusive behaviors, in the end leaving them, like their victims, vulnerable and without the intervention they needed. They were literally accidents waiting to happen.

Clearly, what happened in the summer 2003 in Preston Park could have been anticipated and prevented. For example, the boy considered the ringleader of the attacks was a sixteen-year-old player who was known to have serious discipline problems at school. The grand jury reported, "The high school administrators knew of problems with the students. He had previously threatened teachers and been involved in fights with other students over a two-year period." Vitello reports that members of the team have said that the head football coach, Kevin McElroy, had a special relationship with this sixteen-year-old. McElroy overlooked the boy's fighting because he was a star on the team, they said. McElroy ignored the complaints of the parents of one freshman player who was threatened by the sixteen-year-old just days before camp began. The parents warned Mepham High School's principal, John Didden, about the sixteen-year-old's threat against their son.

Some parents did voice their concern, but in the end there appeared to be no open doors through which the perpetrators, student victims, their peers, concerned parents, and educators could walk to get the intervention and support needed to put an end to this hazing. Everyone involved lost because it seems no one in charge followed film director Gus Van Sant's advice to "look closely." It's the closer look that gets at the problem no one, at school or at home, is noticing.

Why didn't the leaders of the Mepham school community notice that these team leaders were renegades and operating outside the rules of the school community? Did they wonder when it became so easy for the boys not to pay attention to the care, inclusion, and support of the younger newcomers, to become abusers rather than allies? Clearly the school's informal data network, the conversations in the lunchroom, faculty room, hallways, parent coffee klatches, must have contained chatter about the hazing practices that had been in existence for many years. Why didn't the so-called first responders, such as teachers, administrators, support staff, counselors, students leaders, and parent advocates, act?

As in the case of Rob Pace, the intervention of one educator, one adult advocate, or one concerned student who was willing to raise a red flag might have turned this sad incident around before harm was done. The answer, I believe, lies in the lack of expectation by school leaders that informal observations by administrators, counselors, teachers, support staff, students, and parents about students heading for trouble are a critical piece in the development of an effective database for intervention. There appear to have been no open doors through which various members of the school community could walk to share their concerns about these students heading toward the margins. They were, like the three sodomized students, left on their own.

What we have in Mepham is a tragic case of abuse by valued members of the school athletic program, not students who were failing and headed toward dropping out. The insistence of some school administrators, teachers, students, and parents that this kind of behavior can't happen in "our school" compounded this process of turning a blind eye and looking the other way. For example, according to reporter Karla Schuster, "Everyone here is still raw and defensive. Why doesn't anyone talk about the number of students who graduate with Regent's diplomas (83 percent), students and staff say? Or the laundry list of community service projects they do every year, or the two Mepham students named national finalists in the prestigious Siemens Westinghouse competition that honors achievement in math, science. and technology?"[13]

There appeared to be a wall of defensiveness from the school and community rather than a close look at what went wrong. For example, Mepham assistant football coach and gym teacher Art Canestro, in response to a query by reporters Keiko Morris and Karla Schuster, said, "You have to understand that when kids commit crimes against other kids, that's not foreseeable. That's not a foreseeable action. Columbine was not a foreseeable action. The signs weren't there. As teachers, we are very good at reading kids, reading individual's behaviors, and there were no signs that anything was out of the ordinary."[14] However, as Schuster reports, Victor Reichstein, father of a ninth grader on the football team, who has received anonymous threatening letters since he went public with his criticism, suggests, "The school wants to pretend nothing is wrong. It's not civic or school pride for me to rally for people I have no respect for."

In the end, the coach's inability or refusal to "foresee" the hazing problem and read the signs in order to stop this practice resulted in the coaches themselves becoming victims of the assaults. As the *New York Times* reported on March 25, 2004, coaches Kevin McElroy, a social studies teacher, and Art Canestro, a physical education teacher, will continue to work for the district but in administrative jobs where they will have minimal contact with students.[15] Their coaching and teaching careers in tatters, one can only wonder how things would have been different if these coaches were confronted about the abuse and offered intervention and guidance to right this situation, wonder if they, too, had an open door available to walk through to get help. Consider the loss being felt by Coach Canestro, who told reporters Morris and Schuster, "All I can tell you is that I went into the field of teaching because I loved kids. I love to work with kids and I care about kids."[16]

There were lots of victims at Mepham: the sodomized newcomers to the football team and their parents; the educators, support staff, students, and parents who knew about the abuse but remained silent; the perpetrators and their parents who were not confronted and helped; the football coaches who looked the other way and lost their jobs, the support of the community, and probably their own self-esteem; the Mepham High School leadership team who, it seems, looked the other way and put the success of the football team above the safety and well-being of the players; and the school's slogan of "Mepham Pride."

However, James Rullo, a family friend of one of the victims and a critic of the community's failure to help the boys, argues that some good might come out of the experience. Reporter Steve Jacobson reports that Rullo suggests, "Too much was accepted in the past. Maybe this had got some parents awakened to accept the responsibilities to be involved in kids' lives."[17] Clearly the school's intervention strategies need to be expanded to include the athletic standard-bearers and stars who are headed toward the margins and need help, now. And clearly educators, students, and parents need to be expected to act on behalf of students when informal conversations identify students headed toward the margins. But, according to reporter Steve Jacobson, for now Mepham's approach is to add a course in civility to the required physical education program.[18]

"We need to find a way to teach kids the skills to come forward," said Saul Lerner, athletic director at Mepham and the two other schools in the Bellmore district. I would suggest that Mr. Lerner and other educators at Mepham also find ways to open up many doors of help. Leaving it to kids to learn skills isn't enough. We also need educators in the school to fill the role of personal adult advocates for each student—a faculty member who knows the aspirations, strengths, and weaknesses of the student and who can quickly read the signs of emerging trouble from the school's informal and formal data network. What gets measured gets done! In contrast to Coach Conastro's comments, I believe what happened in Columbine and Mepham was foreseeable and avoidable if first responders had used the data that was available to them. Let's remind ourselves of the sound advice of Columbine principal Frank DeAngelis: "The biggest thing that needs to be done nationwide is making sure the kids have a place to go to express themselves and seek help."

THE CASE OF TAYLOR HOOTON

Close friends, teachers, coaches, and parents are important resources in steering students who are headed for trouble into intervention. They are on the front lines and quickly see students headed toward the margins. They can offer initial intervention that can, in some cases, save the lives of students. However, many students, educators, and parents do not see themselves as their brother's keeper. They may see dramatic changes in a student's demeanor, behavior, and emotional/physical well-being, but hesitate to intervene or share their concern with the school's intervention specialist because they fail to trust their own observations and insights that something is going wrong. Billy Ajello is one of those caring high school students. Ajello, a catcher on the Plano, Texas, West Senior High School baseball team, had many concerns about Taylor Hooton, his best friend and pitcher on the team. And his concerns were well placed. On July 15, 2003, a month past his seventeenth birthday, Taylor killed himself. The authorities ruled the death a suicide by hanging.

As writer Jere Longman reports, Taylor's parents and a doctor familiar with the case said that they believe that Taylor's death was related to depression that he felt upon discontinuing the use of anabolic steroids.[19] A sense of euphoria and aggression can be replaced by lethargy, loss of self-confidence, melancholy, and hopelessness when a person stops using performance-enhancing drugs. Dr. Larry W. Gibson, medical director of the Cooper Aerobics Center, a leading preventive medicine clinic in Dallas, said, "It's a pretty strong case that Taylor was withdrawing from steroids and his suicide was directly related to it. This is a kid who was well liked and had a lot of friends, no serious emotional problems. He had a bright future."

Looking back, there were many signals that Taylor was heading for trouble. He was described as a young man who smiled often, was popular with girls, and had many friends from different backgrounds. He was polite and respectful. Blake Boydston, the baseball coach at Plano West, said, "He always came to the field in good spirits. When he spoke, it was, 'Thank you; no, sir; yes, sir.'" And as Ajello said, "You count on the kid to throw strikes."

After Taylor's death, his parents said they had learned from his psychiatrist that he had low self-esteem and that to feel as if he measured up, he had to make himself look bigger, drive a big pickup truck. A junior high coach had also suggested to Taylor that he get bigger, his father, Don Hooton, said. During chemistry class in the fall 2002 Taylor mentioned to Ajello that he might begin using steroids. Ajello asked why and Taylor replied, "I'm not doing it for baseball. I'm doing for myself." There was a dark side to Taylor. Late in the winter and into the spring Don and Gwen Hooton noticed changes in Taylor's physique and behavior. Taylor, who was six feet one and a half inches tall, grew to 205 pounds from about 175 pounds. Initially, his parents did not suspect steroid use. Don Hooton said he felt proud that his son seemed to be working hard in the weight room. Taylor began to develop acne on his back and exhibit signs of aggressiveness and irritability. He flew into rages and then became tearfully apologetic. He took several hundred dollars from his parents' bank account without permission. He would pound the floor with his fists in anger. Once, he punched a wall and injured a knuckle on his pitching hand.

Eventually Taylor's parents became suspicious. He mentioned an interest in steroids and then later confided to his brother, Donald, that he was using them, while still denying it to his parents. His behavior grew more alarming. During a rage in April he told his mother, "I'll just take a knife and end it now."

His parents sent him to a psychiatrist. Taylor told the doctor that he had been injecting himself with the steroid Deca 300 and taking oral Anadrol. By May 19, Taylor said he had stopped using the drugs. But on a trip to England in July, Taylor stole a digital camera and laptop computer, his father said. When his family returned on July 14, his parents, brother, and sister confronted Taylor and told him that his behavior had become unacceptable. He was grounded. The next morning, Taylor asked his mother to lift the punishment but she said no. He went upstairs and, using belts to fashion a noose, hung himself from the door to his bedroom, Don Hooton said. Later, when the police inspected Taylor's room, vials of steroids along with syringes and needles were found. An autopsy revealed the presence of metabolized steroids 19-norandrosterone and 19-noretiocholanolone in Taylor's system, a report from the Collins County Medical Examiner said.

Billy Ajello said he had warned Taylor about the health risks of steroids but that Taylor "kind of blew it off." Apparently none of Taylor's friends alerted an adult. Did Taylor's brother, Donald, intervene to help Taylor once he reported his use of steroids? Clearly Taylor's parents saw the danger and sent him to a psychiatrist. Clearly his close friend Billy Ajello tried to warn him. But it appears no adults or students in the school sensed that Taylor was becoming increasingly troubled. What is needed at the Plano West Senior High Schools of the world are many open doors for intervention, the kinds of open doors that may have saved Taylor's life—open doors through which Taylor himself, his parents, Billy Ajello, concerned coaches, and teachers and peers could walk to get help and share their concerns.

That, as I argue, would entail educating close friends, students, teachers, coaches, and parents that their observations are important and matter. It also means having in place an intervention system that can quickly respond and work closely with a psychiatrist and develop a shared intervention plan that provides a safety net for the Taylors of this world. The issue isn't about blaming school officials, staff, students, or parents for not acting. There is always blame and sometimes denial involved in such cases. Billy Ajello said, "They want to pretend it didn't happen. The administration will probably tell you otherwise but from a student's perspective it's done, it's over with." Phil Saviano, the principal of Plano West, said Taylor Hooton's death was his first encounter with steroids. Mike Hughes, the athletic director and football coach, said, "I have been in the district twenty-one years and I have not known of a kid that was on steroids."[20]

However, the real issue is not about blame but about prevention, the creation of an intervention system in which administrators, counselors, teachers, support staff, students, parents, and community members know their roles, listen, and act when they see another Taylor coming down the road. Taylor's parents learned after his death that he had pummeled his girlfriend's former boyfriend, who required nine stitches to close a wound. Did teachers, coaches, and peers wonder how Taylor broke his knuckle? Did they know he was sometimes out of control and raging? Surely the information about Taylor's new aggressiveness, irritability, and rages was talked about by students, the school nurse, and faculty members.

We need to encourage these significant others to act when they hear about the growing troubles of a student. We need to teach them how to observe and listen and encourage them to use these skills. We need to act on the recommendation of the *Breaking Ranks 11* report that secondary schools provide the Taylors of the world with a personal adult advocate, that is, a faculty member who knew him, who observed his changing physical condition and emotional state, had regular contact with parents Don and Gwen Hooton, acted to make sure the counseling team at Plano West made ongoing contact with his psychiatrist and connected Taylor with ongoing individual and group counseling in the school, and regularly had informal conversations with his friends, such as Billy Ajello, to hear their concerns.

The bottom line is that our schools have to be proactive and responsive, not only reactive as in the example of Plano West High School making counselors available only for its baseball players after Taylor Hooton's suicide. We need to move beyond this kind of intervention that is a one-day, one-shot activity toward an ongoing and more inclusive model. For example, Taylor's friends, classmates, teachers, parents, and coaches also needed help and support to deal with this sudden loss. And principal Phil Saviano and athletic director Mike Hughes probably needed someone to help counsel and guide them through this loss.

THE CASE OF PITCHER NICK ADENHART

In May 2004, Nick Adenhart, a senior at Williamsport High School in Maryland, was ranked as the top-rated high school pitcher in the country. According to writer Dan Steinberg, Adenhart, who had a ninety-five-mile-per-hour fastball and was expected to be a first-round draft pick in the June 2004 baseball draft, a millionaire before his eighteenth birthday.[21] Nick had been a dominant pitcher since Little League. He pitched the Little League all-star team to the state tournament as an eleven-year-old, was untouchable as a twelve-year-old, and had registered in the mid-eighties on a radar gun as a thirteen-year-old. "It was absolutely incredible," said Wayne Main, who coached against a twelve-year-old Adenhart. "I'm telling you, it was him and the catcher and that was all they needed. I mean, you had no chance."

In his junior year, Adenhart was named the Gatorade player of the year in Maryland and then youth player of the year by *Baseball America*. Entering his final season, Adenhart was named by that same magazine as the number-one high school prospect in the country. He signed to play baseball for the University of North Carolina (UNC) in November, but as his draft stock rose, the UNC coaching staff was left "hoping against hope it would ever see Adenhart," according to head coach Mike Fox. Adenhart's high school coach began e-mailing daily updates to a list of three dozen scouts and media members.

The local cable company broadcast two of his starts, the first time it had shown high school baseball. According to Dan Steinberg, Williamsport students gathered to hand "K" signs outside the left field fence, parking lots overflowed with cars, and spectators lined up two to three deep along the foul lines to watch Adenhart pitch. "He's the best I've ever seen," said South Hagerstown's Ralph Stottlemeyer, a high school baseball coach for thirty-five years. Adenhart had never struggled with injuries. He had been on strict pitch counts for the past two years, going past one hundred pitches once or twice. His parents had taken out a considerable insurance policy from Lloyd's of London to guard against career-ending injury. To be safe, Adenhart stopped playing in the field between baseball appearances.

But in mid-May 2004 everything changed for Nick Adenhart. In the final season game against rival South Hagerstown High, facing the third batter of the game, he felt a pop in his elbow, just after throwing a curve. He beckoned longtime catcher David Warrenfeltz to the mound and said he would throw no more curves. But the fastball didn't feel right either. A nod to the dugout brought out Williamsport coach Rod Steiner and, as Dan Steinberg reports, just like that Adenhart was done. Done for the day. Done for the season. Maybe done for life.

The major league scouts at the game, some of whom had traveled from California and Texas, shook their heads in disbelief as they packed up. Adenhart's mother and stepfather rushed to the concession stand, coming back with a bag of ice as scouts scattered with cell phones and the breaking news. Within the next two weeks Adenhart would have two MRI exams. He would fly to Alabama to consult with a famed orthopedist. He would learn of the partial tear in his elbow and what it would take to repair it. John Castleberry, a regional scout for the Texas Rangers, said, "It just shows you how fragile everything is. When you get a good kid like Nick, it's sad."

After a rough few days, Adenhart said he was coming to grips with the situation. "It's a fact you have to accept." He will undergo surgery shortly after graduation and will attend the University of North Carolina and assess his status when he becomes draft eligible again. Adenhart's mother, Janet Gigeous, prefers to talk about the "Carolina Blue Lining," how her son with a 3.2 GPA and 1240 SAT score will be able to experience college, make lifelong friends, and avoid the rigors of a professional baseball career for a few more years. Adenhart's example, she said, can show other high school phenoms not to take their futures for granted.

Nick's story is not unusual. There are many high school athletes throughout the country who have been designated as "stars" and are on the fast track for a scholarship to play at a Division 1 school or move right into the professional ranks. But some of these teens, like Nick Adenhart, do suffer career-ending injuries. Adenhart was done for the day, for the season, and maybe forever with just one pitch.

Suddenly it's over. The accolades, praise, and career and financial possibilities are silenced. But as Adenhart suggests, in some ways he is better off. The pressure is off. "Major league baseball puts you in the situation where you can't turn down the kind of money that I was probably going to get offered. We always wondered how I could do both—get the professional experience of baseball and the relaxed atmosphere of a college experience. Do what most eighteen-year-olds are doing after they graduate. Go to school and plan your life out. Before this I wasn't really sure what was going to happen. The whole draft is a crapshoot. Now I don't really have to worry about the draft. My future is more straight and I know what is going to happen."

It appears that Adenhart is mouthing the right words. Still the pitcher. Always in control. But the new reality he is facing is strange and uncharted territory for him as well as for his parents. He is no longer a star, the treasured commodity of the Williamsport school and community, the maker of headlines and dreams come true. And his parents are no longer at the center of the attention schools and communities bestow on star athletes.

Nick will need intervention to help him sort out how to manage his new life. For the first time, Nick will be seen by others and himself as a person without the baseball glove, not the ninety-five-mile-per-hour fastball pitcher. His intense lifelong involvement with baseball is clearly interrupted and may be over. All the hours devoted to learning the game, conditioning and training, playing on school teams and in summer leagues may now be replaced with emptiness. Hopefully there is an intervention plan available at Williamsport High to offer him support and direction as this new reality sets in, an open door that can help teach him how to relate and respond to peers as the guy without the glove, deal with the loss of what might have been, and help him to not gloss over what he has been forced to give up with statements like, "My future is more straight now and I know what's going to happen." The reality for Nick is that his future is not "more straight" and no doubt he has concerns over "what is going to happen." As Texas Rangers scout John Castleberry reminds us, "It just shows you how fragile everything is." Right now my sense is that Nick Adenhart is feeling the fragility that comes with learning that he is, like all other teens, vulnerable. While the pressure of baseball may be off, the pressure of learning how to handle life without pitching is coming at him like a ninety-five-mile-per-hour fastball.

And I sense his parents will need intervention as well. One can argue that the "Carolina Blue Lining" approach of his mom will be overshadowed by what was lost when Nick felt that pop in his arm, not just the possibilities of fame, financial rewards, and continued accolades but also the intense, all-consuming involvement with their son's sports life that gave their family meaning and purpose. Maybe not right now, but if Nick's injury persists, their new reality will demand attention. For example, where do they put the scrapbook, photos, videos, and newspaper accounts of Nick's performances, the plaques and awards, his gloves and bats, the hundreds of baseballs dated with the score of winning games? They may need help in deciding whether to leave them out around the house, to become yellowed with age, or to tuck them away as memories, out of sight so they don't impede the family's search for a new identity.

And what of Nick's teammates, like longtime catcher David Warrenfeltz? The word "longtime" carries a great deal of meaning. All the games played together in which Nick threw strikes to David suddenly end. No doubt David also feels the loss that came with the pop in the arm, the sudden realization that begins with the words "no more curve balls today." David will need his time to talk and sort out the meaning of Nick's injury. So will coaches like Rod Steiner, who has been a mentor and a major part of Nick's success. Coaches also suffer the feeling of loss when a star player, whom they have nurtured, suddenly can't perform. Like parents, many coaches try to make things turn out right, have a happy ending for their players, but the reality of parental and coaching life is that life can literally throw teens a curve that turns hopes and dreams upside down.

In schools, then, we need to be prepared to respond not only to the trauma and crisis involved in the deaths of a Rob Pace or a Taylor Hooton but also to the sudden shock of star students and athletes like Nick Adenhart. We need to be prepared to help them, their parents, their friends, and concerned faculty members grapple with the changes forced upon their lives. We cannot leave them alone to find their way, gloss over sudden setbacks as no big deal, or allow them to try to move on with their fragile lives mouthing hollow words that mask their real feelings of loss of what might have been.

THE CASE OF THE LATE CALVIN KOHART

There are traumatic events that strike high school students and their parents without warning, events that leave many groups in the school and community searching for support, clarity, and some relief from burdens that are a part of loss. Such was the death by drowning of Calvin Kohart, a popular and athletic fourteen-year-old boy from Wading River, New York, on October 8, 2003.

As reported by writer Tomoeh Murakami Tse, Calvin drowned when a canoe he was in capsized in Wading River.[22] His twin brother, Alfred, and their friend Charles Hoeg, fourteen, were also in the Kohart's family boat about one hundred yards offshore, but were able to make it back to dry land. Calvin was pulled to shore with a rope but was pronounced dead at Central Suffolk Hospital in Riverhead shortly after the 2:00 P.M. incident in the river off the Kohart's waterfront home. Calvin, Alfred, and Charles had the day off from school, Shoreham-Wading River High School. It was a warm October day, with three boys going out on a familiar river to have fun but only two coming back.

Shoreham-Wading River is a small high school of approximately seven hundred students, not the huge high schools that enroll two thousand or more students so commonplace in America. Parents move to the neighboring hamlets of Shoreham and Wading River on the north fork of eastern Long Island to have a safe environment for their kids. They are quiet towns that were once farmland. It's a community in which people know each other through their children's school and athletic events and church. It's a youth-oriented community that encourages academic and athletic excellence from teenagers and, hopefully, admission to the best colleges and universities. Calvin's death connected with me on a personal level: I had started the community's student assistance counseling program in the late 1980s.

In a sense you might say that Calvin had it all, a life many teenagers only dream of. He lived in a home on the water. He had loving parents, Denise and David, who were always present at his games. His dad was also his coach and the cofounder of a youth lacrosse team with Charles Hoeg's father. He was well liked and an athlete and had dreams of attending Princeton University, a Division 1 school, on a lacrosse scholarship. Calvin was a very fortunate teenager. He had hopes, dreams, and possibilities and knew love, caring, and support. He was on the fast track to success. As Dr. Larry W. Gibbons said of Taylor Hooton, "This was a kid who was well liked, had a lot of friends, no serious emotional issues. He had a bright future."

What happens in a community and school when such a sudden and tragic death occurs? Who needs help and support in their effort to make some sense out of this sad event? Clearly, many teenagers and adults in this close-knit school and community are in need. First of all, we have Calvin's parents, Denise and David, who lost a wonderful child who, it seems, was a joy and a gift. There are Calvin's twin brother, Alfred, and friend Charles Hoeg, who witnessed the drowning and who now must come to terms with having survived. There is Charles Hoeg's father, who co-coached the youth lacrosse team with David, traveling frequently to play in out-of-town games and recently winning a tournament in Kentucky. Then there are Calvin's friends, classmates, teachers, coaches, and administrators who valued him.

"Calvin had a zest for life," said Paul Jendrewski, athletic director of the school. Tomoeh Murakami Tse also reports that Calvin's teammates on the lacrosse team said his toughness and skill were so inspirational that he would encourage them to work harder even when they were behind. And as Bernard Thomas, principal of the high school said, "Calvin was a great kid. A loss like this is hard to recover from."

Tragic events such as the death of Calvin Kohart happen regularly in schools and communities all over America. The sudden death of a student by automobile accident, homicide, drug overdose, illness, or suicide quickly changes the focus of the school community, from future events such as college admission to the reality that death is nearby and every member of the community is vulnerable. For students who experience the unexpected loss of a classmate and friend, life is suddenly no longer about sports, SATs, applications to college, dating, and dreaming, as Calvin did, of securing a lacrosse scholarship at Princeton.

There is a new awareness of the vulnerability and risk of life. For teachers and coaches, it often involves a new awareness that all the pressure on students to perform well, pass standardized tests, and get into prestigious colleges and universities doesn't matter in the big scheme of things. And it is also a time when the role of "teacher" means having to address the personal and well-being needs of students impacted by the loss—to be a source of wisdom and strength for students as they grieve, cry, muster up the courage to attend the wake and view the body, say their last good-byes at the funeral, and face the quiet as they return to their homes and gather themselves together for the return to school.

Many students have never been to a wake, seen a dead person, or experienced the emotional roller coaster of the funeral and burial. Many have been unwisely sheltered by parents who chose to "protect" their children from death. They are not prepared and now it falls to caring teachers and counselors to teach them the lessons about death so they are ready when death next enters their lives. These lessons might include walking students through what will be expected at the wake, funeral, and burial; teaching them that showing up, being present, is more important than actual words; standing by them and being a physical and emotional source of support as they work to put their own lives back together; and reminding them that things will not return to normal for a while. This is no easy task for educators, who may themselves be feeling the loss of a student. They, too, need to seek out sources of help and support as they on one hand intervene to guide students in this loss and at the same time are going through many of the same issues that come with sudden death. We often forget that educators have feelings and are vulnerable too.

Calvin Kohart's death serves as a reminder that our schools and communities need many open doors to help those impacted by death and loss. That means creating open doors through which Calvin's parents, Denise and David, his twin brother, Alfred, his friend Charles Hoeg, teachers, administrators, coaches, and counselors themselves can walk to get help in learning how to handle this loss and the ones that will inevitably come in the future. The kind of intervention I am arguing for is, again, proactive, responsive, and ongoing—a system that goes beyond the one-shot counseling sessions offered to students at Shoreham the day after Calvin's drowning, a system that acknowledges that parents, peers, and teachers of all those teenagers like Calvin Kohart who meet an early death also need open doors leading to help and support.

THE CASE OF J. DANIEL SCRUGGS

As reporter Marc Santora tells the story, well before J. Daniel Scruggs, twelve, hanged himself in his closet using one of his neckties, it was clear he was having some kind of trouble.[23] He had failed to show up or was late for school seventy-four out of the past seventy-eight days, complaining that he was being relentlessly bullied. He had taken to defecating and urinating in his pants, rarely washed, and had very bad breath and body odor. Hours after he died in January 2002, the police entered his home in Meriden, Connecticut, and described the home as a total mess where clothes, trash, and debris littered every room. Connecticut state prosecutors criminally charged the boy's mother, Judith Scruggs, in connection with his suicide, claiming her failure to get her son proper counseling put him at undue risk.

During the court proceedings, Melissa Smith, a classmate of Daniel's, testified that he was subjected to relentless bullying at school because he was considered different. "People would spit on his chairs. Sometimes he would ignore it, sometimes he looked like he was going to cry, sometimes he yelled and got into trouble for it." She described times when Daniel was yelled at, punched, kicked, and even thrown off the bleachers in the gym without teachers ever coming to his aid.

His death prompted the creation of an advocacy group for parents and children who are bullied and the passage of a state law requiring that schools develop a system to report bullying. According to Marc Santora, Lisa Toomey, who founded the Advocacy Group for Parents of Children Affected by Bullying, said in an interview, "This country had better swallow and accept the fact that school environments can kill children." The case has drawn national attention because an investigation by the state's child advocate and chief state attorney immediately after the suicide found the boy's complaints about being bullied had gone unanswered. Mrs. Scruggs, a single parent, was found guilty of putting her child at risk and of cruelty to a person.

As in the other cases presented, there is a lot of blame to go around. But here again, as in the case of Rob Pace, Taylor Hooton, and the sodomized Mepham students, the breakdown of help for Daniel is systemic. There appears to have been no intervention system established in the school that could come to the aid of a very troubled boy when his shouts for help must certainly have been heard by educators, peers, and parents. Was anyone, except perhaps classmate Melissa Smith, looking closer?

Keep in mind that it is the closer look that gets at the problem that no one else at home or at school is noticing. Clearly, a teacher, secretary, school nurse, assistant principal, bus driver, hallway monitor, gym teacher, caring peer, or a concerned neighbor must have noticed Daniel's increased fear and struggle. Kids shouldn't have to go to school to be beaten up or return to a home where they are not cared for. There appear to have been no open doors for Daniel to get help and support and no open doors for concerned peers like Melissa Smith, support staff, educators, or parents to share their concern and receive needed advice on how to intervene to help Daniel.

In the end, it appears that Daniel was on his own and lacking any hope that things might change. Enough was enough for this twelve-year-old. Hanging was his way out of the ongoing struggle without help. What a pity. Yes, things might have been different if he were involved in a school community that was ready and set to respond to his many needs. For example, Daniel lacked a personal adult advocate in his school who could have easily observed the troubling data that was emerging and acted to intervene. Daniel's deteriorating march toward the margins of school and community life could have been easily tracked through his tardiness, truancy, lack of physical and emotional well-being, and being the target of relentless bullying. Who knew of his aspirations, strengths, and weaknesses?

It appears that teachers failed to convey a sense of caring for Daniel and engage his family as partners in his education, as advocated in the *Breaking Ranks 11* report. And it appears that the school failed to follow the *Breaking Ranks 11* suggestion to successfully interact with hard-to-reach parents with activities such as home visits, Saturday meetings, and meetings outside of regular business hours. Mrs. Scruggs was also on her own without help and support. Where was the connection between the school and agencies in the community to help coordinate the delivery of physical and mental health and social services for Daniel and his mom?

Imagine what the educators, support staff, students, and parents in Daniel's school are feeling in the aftermath of his hanging, knowing what they knew, having the data, and somehow failing to act. It is a bit like seeing a house on fire and failing to act, not looking closely, just walking by. Hopefully there is a new approach in that school so that when another Daniel appears there is a closer look at the problem. It is the closer look and intervention that might have saved the lives of Rob Pace, Taylor Hooton, and J. Daniel Scruggs. It is the closer look and intervention that might have averted the sodomizing at Mepham High. It is the closer look at Nick Adenhart that reminds us that care and attention need to be paid to our fallen student heroes, who may appear strong and stalwart but who are in reality teens coping for the first time with their vulnerability. It is the closer look at the impact of Calvin Kohart's drowning that offers the data that in addition to his parents, his friends, peers, support staff, teachers, administrators, other parents, and counselors themselves need help and support.

This informal data-gathering process enables school leaders to take that necessary closer look at each student, monitor their behavior, and quickly intervene when necessary. This process serves as an extension of the formal data, the SWP-gathering process I described earlier in this chapter, and adds a human connection, a real face and story, to the numbers. In a sense, both a formal and informal data gathering complement each other and provide the basis for intervention.

What I am arguing for in this informal data-gathering process is that educators avoid, as physician Lisa Sanders suggests, the tendency in medicine to focus on the data about the patient, the vital signs, the monitors, the labs, and instead focus on the patient himself or herself.[24] As Dr. Sanders reports, "We look after patients without looking at them." Our data-gathering process in the school needs to begin with knowing each student well by "looking at them" every day and using our observations to act quickly when there are signs of trouble.

As researchers Robert L. Sinclair and Ward J. Ghory (1990) advise, part of this work of "looking" is for educators to concern themselves with students in retreat. Retreating students are reluctant to maintain a charade of acceptable behavior. When they can, they reject not only the school's goal but also the available means of learning. The truant, the selective class cutter, the chronically tardy student, the pupils caught smoking in the bathrooms or hanging out behind the stairs—these are the young people who withdraw to the margins of situations they see as increasingly hopeless or absurd. Their perceptions are generally confirmed when parents or school officials stigmatize and punish them without providing avenues for productive participation. They hold fiercely to their peers as their support in a turbulent, threatening environment. Sinclair and Ghory remind us that when these students are labeled and stigmatized by the school, they are further cut off from constructive aspects of their past and from positive, potential abilities they may have.

In this aggressive, defensive, self-protective, negative cycle, the assertive trappings of marginal status lead to students being dealt with as if they were, and had always been, only their current public identities.[25] I would also suggest that in looking for students in retreat we need a data-gathering process that moves beyond focusing only on students who are class cutters, truants, and bathroom smokers, and includes those students who are quietly in retreat—for example, the student who hangs out after school each day to avoid going home to an alcoholic parent, literally being forced to leave; the student who shows signs of anorexia, has lost fifty pounds but continues a regimen of working out for two hours after school and then running five miles; or the student who is trying, but failing, to move beyond his junior high label as being a troublemaker and from a mixed-up family, the kind of teen who has always been among "the usual suspects" when mischief occurs but now wants to fit in while the old label continues on, his search for a new identity continuously tripped up by his past record.

This looking at students needs to include building trusting relationships with them. In my experience in the schools, I have found teens will tell educators and support staff their stories and share data about themselves if they find someone who is available, will listen, respects their lives, offers what Sinclair and Ghory call "avenues for productive participation," and can be trusted.

Researchers Anthony S. Bryk and Barbara Schneider, professors at the University of Chicago, suggest that the bedrock of trust between educators and students rests on four supports: respect, competence, integrity, and personal regard for others.[26] They describe their work as about "not forgetting the people," that is, not to forget that each child is looking for a way of being a productive part of the school community and our role as educators is to help them find that "avenue for participation," an avenue that is made clearer by knowing the stories and data about each child. The data provide us with the road map to inclusion, participation, and, when needed, intervention.

The case studies of Rob Pace, the Mepham High School football players, Taylor Hooton, and J. Daniel Scruggs strongly convey the message of what can happen if educators are focused only on grades and test scores and do not "look" at their students each day. These sad events need not take place if educators pay attention to both the formal and informal data about students that is readily available, data that can help them be ready and set to intervene to help students headed toward the margins. This data-gathering process must be governed by the need to construct a clear picture of what is going on in the lives of each student, right now, and used to respond quickly to any movement toward the margins.

THE MANY SOURCES AND RESOURCES IN THE SCHOOL AVAILABLE TO GATHER INFORMAL DATA ABOUT STUDENTS AND THEIR FAMILIES

Here is a list of potential data-gathering resources available in every school that, each in its own unique way, contributes to the student's being known:

- *The School Principal.* The principal should be viewed as the lead person in the data-gathering process. He or she needs to send the message to professional and support staff, students, and parents that observations about students heading toward the margins are an important and expected part of their unique contribution to the school community. Principal Doug Lowery Jr., from Hilliard Memorial School, is a good example of such an administrator. As reported by education writer Carla Smith, if you stop by his office, he probably won't be there. Instead, you might find him dishing up lunch in the school cafeteria, playing football with students in the playground, or spending some time in the classroom.[27] Lowery is no ordinary principal. He's a hands-on administrator who can boast that he knows every student by his or her first name and whose educational focus is not only on student achievement but also on ensuring that personalization is part of the process.

According to Sam Di Salvo, assistant principal at Hilliard Memorial, "Doug's contribution to this school building, if I had to put it into one word, is simply presence. Lowery's priority is to make his presence known." According to Di Salvo, that means visibility in the hallways, visibility in the classrooms, efforts to know the pieces and parts that go into after-school activities or before-school activities, a genuine interest in everything that requires his presence. Lowery uses one word to describe his leadership style: personalization. It's that one-on-one contact with students, teaching staff, and community members that makes him a leader. "I spend a great deal of time with kids and with teachers trying to support them. Without personalization, we don't know kids, we really don't know our staff, and our performance isn't going to be positive. This is a job all about commitment. If you are going to do it right, you need to take time to help kids. I know every student's name to make sure they feel connected to the school and us. They are known, not just educated."

Clearly, Doug Lowery would have taken a more personal approach to the Rob Pace situation, the ongoing bullying at the Mepham football camp, Taylor Hooton's steroid use, and the bullying of J. Daniel Scruggs and Judith Scruggs's seeming neglect of her child. He notices and acts.

• *Teachers.* Teachers on the front lines can easily spot changes in a student's behavior, physical and emotional well-being, and level of energy and motivation. Teachers are key members of the school's data-gathering team. They are ideally positioned to make themselves available to students, listen to their stories, respect and understand these stories, develop trust, and guide them toward open doors that offer credible sources of help and support. In short, teachers are capable of offering powerful relationships.

Eliot Levin, special project director for the Big Picture Company, a nonprofit organization that creates personalized schools and systems to support them, reports on the value of expecting teachers to become personally involved with all aspects of their students' lives.[28] He offers as evidence of the value of such personal support the example of the Met School, a small urban public high school in Providence, Rhode Island, where the emphasis on strong relationships makes student learning more engaging, relevant, and enduring.

At the Met School each student has an advisor and is a member of an advisory, a model I would suggest from *Breaking Ranks 11* report recommending a personal adult advocate for each student. The advisory group is made up of fourteen students led by the teacher/advisor who works closely with students throughout all four years of high school. The advisory is a small, supportive group, an extended family, in which all students are known well. Advisors touch base with every student daily and schedule frequent one-on-one meetings to plan, implement, and evaluate each student's learning.

According to Levin, over time advisors become deeply familiar with each student's abilities, needs, and interests, which allows them to help each student learn. Advisors also come to know their students' families through frequent phone conversations, school events, and quarterly meetings during which parents help plan their children's curriculum and assess their progress. The strong ties that Met teachers forge with students' families help prevent student dropout and gang involvement, allow teachers to mediate family problems that disrupt students' learning, and encourage the development of a powerful school community in which teachers and parents work together to promote student achievement. Of course, not every school has the resources to develop an advisory program based on the Met School model.

But teachers can be personal adult advocates and carry out many of the components in the advisory program, such as creating strong relationships; knowing their students well; touching base with students on a regular basis; becoming deeply familiar with students' abilities, interests, and needs; knowing their students' families through frequent phone conversations, school events, and meetings; helping mediate family problems that disrupt students' learning; and encouraging the development of a powerful school community in which teachers and parents work together to promote student achievement. Teachers who are personally engaged in each of these activities are ideally positioned to observe students and assess the data needed for intervention when troubles arise.

- *Concerned Students Coupled with Available and Skilled Counselors.* Students are vital resources in identifying peers headed for trouble. They live on the front lines of the school and know what is going on with their peers. It is important to create the expectation in the school that their observations and feedback are an important part of the school's intervention program.

However, concerned students need a go-to person to connect with when they observe a peer headed for trouble. Students should not have to carry the burden of knowing about a peer's trouble and find no open door, no arena of comfort, through which they can walk to share their concerns and the burden that comes with knowing, as was the case with student Melissa Smith in the J. Daniel Scruggs case. Schools need to have a skilled and well-trained counselor whose major role is to be available, visible, knowable and to serve as a resource, an open door, for concerned students and students headed for trouble by offering individual and group counseling.

Here is an example of how that process can work. In the late 1980s, I was involved in developing a student assistance–counseling role in Shoreham-Wading River High School in eastern Long Island. This role emerged from the need to address a growing number of personal issues affecting students and parents. Wisely, the role was presented as an add-on to the guidance department, not as a separate, competitive agency.

In a sense, the role was a natural extension of a guidance department that had its hands full with the tasks of testing, scheduling, and college admissions, leaving them with little time or priority to offer individual and group counseling. Therefore, the student assistance–

counseling role was able to get off the ground with no resistance from counselors who found themselves in the position of dealing with criticism from parents, teachers, students, and administrators that they were neglecting the growing need for personal counseling for students. It was a good first step.

In the first year of developing this counseling approach, my work was not unlike that of Hilliard principal Doug Lowery. I spent a great deal of time in the hallways and cafeteria, greeting students as they arrived in the morning and as they left in the afternoon, at athletic events, and at dances. I made myself available and visible, and in the process let students know me as a person as well as a professional—the father of five boys, two of whom attended a nearby high school and competed with Shoreham in baseball and basketball. I also played basketball and ran with students after school. In this process, I was in a position to hear the stories of who was partying, who got drunk or drugged up, whose parents were divorcing, and so on, as well as the good news of achievements and winning games. I knew from my past experience in beginning new programs that visibility was the key first step in building this counseling process. I, like Doug Lowery, worked to know what was going on and made my presence known, to show that I was available, knew students by name, knew their hopes and aspirations, and was informed about their school, home, and social life. I conveyed that I wanted to be of help and support and would respect their privacy and value their trust. You have to believe, as I did, that as a counselor you have something worthwhile to offer students and you can be counted on to deliver help, no matter how painful the problem.

Within a short time, that personalization process began to pay off in self-referrals by students; referrals from teachers, administrators, support staff, and parents; referrals from students concerned about a peer. One of these concerned students was Kathy M. Kathy was a senior who had a locker just outside my office. One day after school she asked if we could talk. She was visibly upset and had been crying. My response was a simple request (simple questions work best for teens)—"talk to me about what is going on." She reported that Rob, her best friend, had been cutting himself with a razor blade over the past three months and she was afraid he was suicidal. She reported that Rob had sworn her to secrecy about the cutting but that she just couldn't keep it to herself any longer. "What should I do?" she asked. I reassured her that seeking out help for Rob and herself was the best course and, yes, I could help.

In a sense I wasn't surprised by Kathy's concerns. I had noticed that Rob—the shoo-in class valedictorian, four-year honor student, class president, taking three Advanced Placement (AP) courses, son of a school board member and elementary teacher—had appeared very unhappy, even desperate, in the hallways. I had overheard talk about pressure from his father, the school board member, and mother to get into an Ivy League school.

Rob was clearly the standard-bearer for the school, someone students and staff and community members pointed to as an example of the school district's accomplishments. But as Kathy said, he suddenly couldn't keep up. He started missing classes and assignments, lost his appetite, and began cutting himself on his arms and legs. As Kathy described the situation, it was not difficult for me to see that Rob was heading for trouble, and on the fast track. His only source of help was Kathy, who was burdened herself with this situation and needed intervention as well. So Kathy and I hatched an intervention plan.

First, she would tell Rob that she was extremely concerned about him, that he needed more help and she could no longer honor his request not to tell anyone about his cutting himself. It was just too much of a burden to carry around every day. I also asked Kathy to tell Rob that she had talked to me about the situation and convey the message that I wanted to help and that our discussion would be private.

Rob and Kathy did show up the next afternoon after most students had departed for home. I believed that if I had a few minutes to talk with Rob, we could make some inroads on his problem. I felt if I failed on this first overture I would keep trying for a breakthrough. Part of this decision, of course, had another perspective. Should I call his parents and alert the school principal right now, before I had a chance to meet with Rob?

I decided to hold on that move but nevertheless I was anxious. As Rob began to tell his story, Kathy holding his hand and offering encouragement, what came through was all the tiredness of being the standard-bearer for too long. From the beginning days in elementary school, Rob was always on the honor roll, seen as the best and brightest, groomed for the Ivy Leagues and success in life, the most likely to succeed. He was always preparing and studying, with no time, no license, to just hang out, miss assignments, fail, say "fuck it" to all the demands of his parents, the school, and the bully inside him that said "don't idle."

He talked often of wanting to change places with the kids who hung out in the back of the school, who smoked and didn't care about school. They went home each night with no books, watched dumb stuff on the TV, and hung out with girls. He talked of being forced into the spotlight, of being the do-good son of a school board member and a teacher who thrived on his successes and recorded his every achievement on video and in a scrapbook. The three AP courses in his senior year finally did him in. He said it "became so overwhelming," the courses, the college applications, essays, college visits, the never-ending talk of scholarships, and, just recently, what graduate school he might attend.

His dad was pushing premed and his mom engineering. "It all got out of hand," he said. He began to cut himself in the fall and said in some ways it helped him get through the day. He said some of his teachers noticed he was lax in turning in assignments but no one seemed to really notice his unhappiness, tiredness, or retreating. He said plaintively, "All people notice about me is my awards and achievements; they don't see me as a person. Everyone is counting on me to get into Harvard or Princeton, that's all. They don't care if I am unhappy. Not even my parents. They are like my managers, not my parents. If they knew how I was feeling, what I was doing to myself, that I was here talking to you, they'd be shocked. 'Not my kid' kind of thing. I'm just tired. I don't even want to go to college next year. I don't even want to pass those AP courses. Even without those courses I have more than enough credits to graduate in June. I just want to stop, get off this crazy trip. But I don't know how. Can you help me?"

And so the real Rob, his long-quieted voice, came to be known to himself, Kathy, and me. He was ready and set for help and, in a sense, a plan of his own. He didn't want to go to college next year or finish his AP courses. He wanted help and some time out. He wanted his parents to understand and begin to love him and care for him as the young kid he was, not the achiever. And he wanted his teachers and classmates and neighbors to just let him be for a while. Lastly he wanted to learn how to be a normal teenager, hang out and have fun.

We decided on an intervention plan. I would contact Rob's parents and he and I would meet with them that evening. I would also contact a physician colleague at a local hospital that offered a three-month treatment intervention for adolescents who self-harm and set up a tentative appointment for Rob and his parents. I would accompany them to the appointment if Rob thought it would help. And if all went well, with the permission of Rob and his parents, I would consult with school administrators to work out a three-month withdrawal for Rob in which he would drop his three AP courses but continue his other course work while at the hospital. My role would be to maintain weekly contact with Rob, his parents, and the hospital, keeping communication open and planning Rob's reentry. Finally, Kathy and I would continue counseling.

And so the plan evolved. Rob's parents were upset but they, too, had a sense that something was wrong and admitted that the pressure of always promoting Rob's success was taking its toll on the family and their marriage. They seemed relieved and hopeful that the hospital intervention would help Rob. As Rob's mother said, "Maybe we can get our son back and we can start over." Rob and his parents, after consulting with my physician colleague, did enter a three-month rehab program for depression and self-harm.

After his rehab Rob returned to school in the spring and graduated. He didn't get into Harvard or Princeton. He wasn't even valedictorian. Instead, he enrolled as a dramatic major at a local university and got involved in acting. He's now on Broadway. Kathy, too, learned a valuable lesson about helping. You can't, and shouldn't have to, carry someone else's problems and burdens. It's OK to ask for help for yourself as well as for the troubled person.

As physician Lisa Sanders advises, there is a tendency in medicine, and I say in the schools, to focus on the data about the patient—the vital signs, the monitors, the labs—rather than on the patient himself or herself. We look after patients instead of looking at them. Our work in developing an effective intervention that can respond to the

Robs in our schools needs to include easily accessible open doors through which the Kathys can walk, tell their stories, and get help. This intervention system needs to be focused on knowing and understanding Rob as a person, not just the standard-bearer who can always be counted on to excel; to notice the changes taking place in Rob's behavior; to act; to relieve Kathy of carrying this burden by herself and to pass on the lessons learned from Rob's case as a warning to future Robs that harm can come from too much pressure to succeed.

- *School Nurses*. The school nurse's office probably offers more formal and informal data about students than any other agency in the schools, that is, if—and it's a big if—the school nurse is accessible, available, listens well, and, when necessary, confronts, provides credible advice and referral, and is a source of support when troubles arrive for high school teens. And they do, in spades.

Sue Maguire, principal of the Molly Stark School in Bennington, Vermont, is right on target when she says, "The school's job is academic, but we can't ignore that physical and mental well-being of kids is tied to academics."[29] School nurses are the go-to persons in the school to identify well-being problems in their early stages. They are often the professionals who first notice teens affected by eating disorders such as anorexia or bulimia or obesity; tobacco, drug, or alcohol addiction; sexual, physical, or emotional abuse issues; or family conflicts such as divorce and isolation. Multiple issues, such as parents' divorce, a smoking addiction, and truancy, often affect many of the students who find a haven in the nurse's office. These are the teens, aptly described by researchers Simmons and Blyth (1987), who simultaneously experience a number of life changes, such as a move from junior high to high school, pubertal change, early onset of dating, change of residence, or change in parents' marital status. Change comes too suddenly for these students. Life is not easy.

The good news is that many of these students find arenas of comfort and guidance in conversations with inviting, accessible, and caring school nurses. As Simmons and Blyth (1987) suggest, if the individual is comfortable in some environments, life arenas, and role relationships, then discomfort in other arenas can be tolerated and mastered. There needs to be some arena of life or some set of role relationships with which the student can feel relaxed and comfortable, to which he or she can withdraw and become invigorated.

In my observations of many school nurses, what comes through is the ability of many of these professionals to provide such a safe and caring haven for students. An approachable school nurse hears many intimate, sometimes alarming, conversations during their daily work in our large secondary schools. These conversations range from possible suicide, drug overdose, fear of pregnancy, conflicts with family and relationships, illness related to smoking and poor diet, the pressures of the college admission process, physical abuse by a boyfriend, anxiety and confusion over the sudden death of a classmate like Rob Page, Taylor Hooton, and J. Daniel Scruggs, discussion of the injury to Nick Adenhart and the detour of his major league dreams, or the sodomizing of the Mepham High School football players. These conversations usually begin with a simple question by the nurse, such as "How is it going?" or "You look upset. Let's talk" and often result in a referral to a school counselor, physician, or community mental health person and involvement of the student's parents.

The nurse's office in many schools is a place teens want to be, a chosen destination, a respite from troubles and a place to receive real advice, advice that is not always welcome but is right on target. It is a place where, students understand, they can expect challenge and confrontation if they continue to not care for themselves and act out with destructive behaviors and addictions.

Lorraine Esper, a registered nurse and school nurse at Shoreham-Wading River High School, is one of those special nurses with a gift of being able to relate to teens headed for trouble. A trusted colleague, she was a partner in helping me to develop the student assistance program at the school. Her office was strategically located next door to mine. I spent many class periods in there in conversations with students, conversations that often resulted in a self-referral or a plea to help a classmate in trouble. In turn, Lorraine would often pop into my office with a student in tow, asking if I had a few minutes to help out. We were an efficient team with the common goal of providing an arena of comfort for students.

Lorraine's being a major asset to the school and its students is easily explained. She is ready and set to listen to students as they arrive for the beginning of school. By 7:15 A.M. her office is filled with students talking to her, often in small groups, about health and well-being issues. Some students drop by to leave their cigarettes, so they are not tempted to smoke during the school day. They were part of the twenty-seven-member student smoker group Lorraine and I had developed and that I have described briefly in an earlier publication.

The program, aptly named the Five-Hour-a-Day Smoking Reduction Group, was designed to help students get through the school day without smoking and learn how to make better lifestyle choices.[30] The twenty-seven students were divided into three small groups that met with Lorraine and me once a week for ten weeks. The topics included who is in charge of your smoking, improving your self-image, stress factors that trigger smoking, the power of addiction, related addictions such as alcohol or drugs, rewarding ourselves in ways other than smoking, and developing a plan for a healthier lifestyle.

A side benefit of the Five-Hour-a-Day program was the entry of some students into rehab for addictions and others enrolling in a peer counseling program I developed where they could help younger students on the road to addiction. The program was, as Sinclair and Ghory (1990) suggest, an effort to create an avenue of participation for students headed toward the margins of school life, many of whom had lost sight of their own self-worth and the constructive elements of their own past behaviors and achievements.

Up to now many of the student smokers had been labeled as future dropouts who visibly challenged school rules and the healthy lifestyles of their peers. However, what we learned was that many addicted students wanted to stop smoking and were looking for alternatives and wanted to be included in the larger school community, to be invited in and valued, and to use the lessons learned in their recovery process to help other students. They were tired of being left alone, isolated, in retreat on the outside, looking in. Lorraine and I also teamed up to develop the 48-Hour Alcohol Support Group and an eating disorder group. The 48-Hour group involved students learning how to get through the weekend without drinking, a major problem for many high school students, high achievers, and student athletes in particular, who lead healthy lives during the week but use and abuse alcohol on the weekends. The eating disorder group involved students who were anorexic or bulimic and was connected to community health resources for referral and education.

The kinds of conversations I describe earlier and possible connections with a wide variety of support groups continue throughout the day and after school. There seems to be no let up for Lorraine, no down time. She is "on" all day long. Lorraine is an excellent and inviting listener but her involvement doesn't stop there. She is quick to offer advice, referrals, and follow-up support. She doesn't shy away from confrontation. If she feels a student needs more help with a problem she is very skilled at selling, prodding a student toward a referral. She doesn't turn a blind eye to students in trouble. Like principal Doug Lowery, Lorraine personalizes each student relationship. She knows the student's name, family background, school performance, social life or lack of it, and issues the student is trying to resolve. I believe one can say that J. Daniel Scruggs might still be alive if he were in Lorraine's school, and Judith Scruggs would have connected with the support she needed, not be serving time in jail and thinking of where it all went wrong for her family.

But there is a downside in the role of caring school nurses. They are often overwhelmed by the demands of needy students. They often don't have the time and opportunity to share their observations about students headed toward the margin with other educators and administrators, data they need to have in order to plan effective intervention strategies. The data remains locked in the nurse's office. Clearly the nurse's presence and modeling of skillful involvement with students and establishing a safe comfort arena works, but the reality is that they are individual persons trying to respond to many needs.

I believe most effective school nurses find themselves in a similar position, responding to the many needy students who walk through their open doors all day long and at the same time searching for ways to raise the level of care and education they can provide, such as short-term drug counseling, education on healthy lifestyle choices, and encouraging students to take responsibility for their personal health and health care, while being aware that there are students in the school who need intervention but are hesitant to reveal their concerns. Nurses can interact with only so many students each day. How might they reach more students and take on a more educational and prevention role? There are alternatives.

Here is an example of the possibilities available using the school nurse model as the pillar of the program. Carolyn Ahl and a group of student nurses at the University of Washington School of Nursing participated in a ten-week clinical rotation at Cleveland High School in Seattle, which serves a student body of 750 ethnically diverse and economically disadvantaged teens in grades nine through twelve.[31] As part of this rotation, they developed a health promotion Internet site to enhance health education and provide a source of confidential information for students that was available to every student at Cleveland. The site was named the Teen Smart Web.

One of the exercises in the Teen Smart Web is Ask a Nurse. The program was designed to give students a private and confidential forum to discuss health questions with the school's nurse. Individual student's questions are published and answered anonymously on the website. Teen Smart also has a Frequently Asked Questions section so that all students could benefit from the information. The questions that students pose online are much more likely to address health concerns of a sensitive nature, for example, sex and drugs. The Teen Smart site also includes a Discussion Board that provides students with the opportunity to analyze common life situations where decision making is crucial to health and safety. Each week the discussion board presents a problem-based scenario on topics such as drinking and driving, having unprotected sex, or using illicit drugs. Individual students can post a response describing what they would do in a given situation and also view other students' responses.

• *Coaches.* Coaches are also a valuable source of informal data about students. They come in contact with students and parents in a very intimate and intense way and sometimes, unlike the Mepham coaches' situation, that relationship enables students to develop a close personal bond with coaches and share personal problems. Think about Williamsport baseball coach Rod Steiner and the important role he can play in counseling Nick Adenhart, his parents, and teammate David Warrenfeltz. Here is a very vivid example of the power of those kinds of relationships and the lessons that students can learn about life.

Chris P., a senior at Shoreham-Wading River High School, was full of hope. This would be his year and his team's year to win the 1992 Suffolk County basketball championship. This year's team was composed of veteran seniors who had been slowly brought along by coach Cliff Lennon. Now they were ready. But, as I described briefly in an earlier publication, there was a worry that clouded this optimism and it involved the deteriorating health of his beloved coach Lennon, a math and science teacher at the middle school.[32] Cliff had come to the district in 1985 after a successful twenty-year career as an engineer.

Within a year of his hiring, Lennon had made his mark. He coached the girls' softball team and the boys' lacrosse team at the middle school and became head basketball coach at the high school. He was filled with energy and a zest for helping students. He arrived at school an hour before classes to tutor students and advise them on personal problems. After school he would coach from 4:00 to 6:00 P.M. On many nights he would stay on to tutor and advise students and meet with parents. He regularly chaperoned social functions at the middle school and high school and served as a faculty advisor on field trips.

Lennon seemed to be always available, helping and advising students. He even gave out his home phone number to students and encouraged them to call him with academic and nonacademic problems. Students at both the middle school and the high school flocked to him for advice and support.

Students found him, as a coach, to be a winner who encouraged student athletes to be all they could be. But he could also be tough and confrontational when those skills were needed to prod a reluctant student or athlete. He made believers out of senior players like Chris P. who were returning for the 1991–1992 season. He preached that this was their year and they could take the county championship. Cliff was also particularly focused on helping female students and athletes take their places as leaders in the school. He gave 100 hundred percent of himself and the students appreciated it.

By 1990 Cliff had established a reputation as a gifted and caring teacher, advisor, and winning coach, a colleague who was dedicated to helping students and who, like Lorraine Esper, noticed students headed for trouble and quickly intervened with works of support, advice, and referral. I had been instrumental in encouraging Cliff to apply for the Shoreham position and, as a longtime friend, was thrilled at his great success. He had found a second career, a home really, in Shoreham, where he could do his work—helping kids.

But the halcyon days of the late 1980s began to change for Lennon. The 1991 basketball team won the league title but lost out in the county finals. Many of the games were close and hard fought. After the season ended, Cliff told me he was thinking of giving up coaching basketball. He reported that he felt burned out by the rigors of the season. He was experiencing severe stomach pains and did not feel well. He appeared tired, sickly, forcing himself to keep up with the regimen he had set for himself. It was hard for me and others in the school community to watch a gifted teacher and coach like Cliff, who was always available, caring, and responsive, become ill. Like many of his students I was angry. Life should not be this way.

But I knew from my counseling and personal life experience that we all get hit by life's blows. Cliff's life was no exception. The results of a medical check-up proved to be more serious than the need to give up coaching. He was diagnosed with colon cancer. At first Cliff approached the disease the way he approached his life. He told me he would beat the cancer and he didn't want others to worry about him. But he could not handle it himself. He was already seriously ill.

By springtime some students, staff, and parents suspected something was not right with him. He was clearly having trouble keeping up with his rigorous daily routine of teaching, advising, and coaching. Rumors about his health spread through the school community. In late spring Cliff and I sat down and helped make a plan for dealing with his deteriorating condition. He decided he had to talk to the students, staff, and parents about his illness. He said he felt he owed the truth to the people who cared about him and he realized there would be questions he had to answer. Should he step down as basketball coach and let someone else take over? Planning for a summer basketball camp had to take place by June. How could he continue to handle his teaching assignments if he was going to miss days for chemotherapy treatments and medical visits? How could he communicate the seriousness of his illness to his own sons?

Cliff was fortunate to have a support group to whom he could turn for help. He talked with his teaching team, assistant basketball coaches, principals at the middle and high schools, school nurse, athletic director, and me. As a result of his open communication and asking for help, the middle school principal hired a permanent substitute to help Cliff in the classroom. The school nurse advised him on medical issues and set up a program that brought a prepared meal to his family each night. Cliff explored coaching options with athletic director Mike Schwenk. Cliff's teaching team, as well as the counselors in the middle and high schools, made an effort to provide counseling and support for the many students, staff members, and parents affected by Cliff's illness, as well as for his two sons. The idea that Cliff might die began to sink in within the school community.

By summer Cliff had trouble handling the demanding schedule of a basketball camp and traveling to scrimmages. In the fall voices inside the middle and high schools could be heard talking about the possibility of his dying before the year was out. Mike Schwenk asked me for advice on how to talk to Cliff about taking on a co-coach to help him with his basketball duties. He wanted to have support ready to help the team members, all of whom were close to Cliff.

Ironically, this 1991–1992 team promised to be Coach Lennon's best team ever, a team he had nurtured and developed for four years. Mike Schwenk wanted to approach Sal Mignano, the middle school health teacher and high school baseball coach, about being a co-coach. Schwenk's well-thought-out and caring plan was to let Cliff take the lead and let Mignano take over slowly as the coach's health deteriorated. This plan would allow Cliff the dignity of making a decision to step down on his own when the time came. Schwenk approached Cliff and sold him on the idea, suggesting Mignano for the job. When the news was announced to the basketball team, they breathed a sigh of relief. They were in good hands with Mignano aboard and a winning and dedicated coach like Lennon. Support continued to be put in place that gave Lennon dignity and his student athletes the mentors they could depend on. Students, staff, and parents jumped on board to help and didn't duck the hard choices to be made. That process seemingly took the burden off Cliff. He now could give himself permission to be tired and ill. It was not what we all wanted for him but it was what was—the coming death of a dear friend, mentor, colleague, coach, father, and father figure to many students.

By mid-December the team was in first place and playing with great skill and courage. Team members dedicated the season to Coach Lennon. They were going to win the league and county championships for him. Anxiety among students, staff members, and parents seemed to diminish as clear evidence of support for Cliff began to take hold. He was not on his own and neither were they. By Christmas, Cliff was very ill. The high school principal, along with myself and members of the Kids in Need Committee (an intervention team made up of the principal, school psychologist, social worker, counselors, nurse, teacher representative, community outreach person, and myself) began planning a crisis response with key teachers, counselors, and student leaders in the event of Cliff's death. In early January, Cliff was hospitalized. The support system continued to work in the hospital room with students, staff, and parents making regular visits.

Meanwhile, the basketball team continued to win. Each evening after practice of a game, Mignano and the assistant coaches would arrive at the hospital to tell Cliff about the team's progress, a major time and emotional commitment on their part. Back at the high school and middle school, students, staff, and parents were kept informed about Cliff's condition and encouraged to share their feeling about his loss from the school scene. In class discussions and counseling groups, some involving the team players, many students voiced great anxiety over his increasingly grave condition and about death in general. Questions abounded. What is death? Are there a heaven and a hell? Many of the students had never been to a wake or funeral. They voiced concern about viewing a dead body, especially that of Mr. Lennon. Some students were angry with a God who could make a good person so ill. Meanwhile, the basketball team clinched the league title and was in the playoffs.

Cliff Lennon died on January 27, 1992. The high school and middle school response plan was in place. But no matter how carefully and thoughtfully a school prepares for a crisis, it still comes as a shock. Both school principals announced over the public address systems that Mr. Lennon had died. There would be no hiding the event or keeping people out of the loop. Everyone was to be informed. Many students, staff, and parents had been on this journey with Cliff; now they needed to be included as the journey came to an end.

The high school principal praised Mr. Lennon for his many contributions to the school. He also thanked everyone for their ongoing support and provided information about the wake and funeral. Buses would be available to take any interested students and staff to the funeral. Substitutes would be hired to cover classes. He indicated that in the few days preceding the funeral, students were expected to attend classes but teachers could turn these classes into discussion groups about Mr. Lennon and the issues involved in death. He also indicated that counseling groups would be set up in the offices of the student assistance counselor, school nurse, counselors, and school psychologist for students and staff in need of extra support. A counseling group for parents would be set up in the school library.

The planning for Cliff's good-bye was not without its bureaucratic battle for turf that is so much a part of any organization. Cliff, being a professional in both the middle school and high school, had a divided audience. Which school did he "belong" to? Which school had the privilege of being called "Cliff's school"? Fortunately these turf battles, not unlike the family infighting that occurs in deciding who has the final decision about details when burying a divorced person who has anchors in two families, were addressed. Thankfully the logic of the expression "let the dead bury the dead" prevailed. The reality was that Cliff was connected to and belonged to everyone—students, staff, and parents—not to a school. He gave them hope and a deep sense of connecting to a community where kids matter, regardless of grade.

The basketball team was scheduled to play in the county playoffs on the day of Cliff's wake. Some staff members and parents wanted the game postponed but the coaches argued, "Coach Lennon would want us to play. What better gift could we bring to the wake than a victory?" The game went on and the team won. They had made it to the final county championship game. When the team arrived at the wake, they were greeted with quiet applause and hugs. As the team members passed before Coach Lennon's coffin, one could sense their pride in winning this one for the coach. It seems like playing, winning, and continuing to take things day by day had given them the courage to deal with, and accept, his death.

The funeral proved to be a release. More than half the student body of the middle school and high school attended. The basketball team served as pallbearers. Many students, staff, and parents eulogized Cliff. A community paid its respects and taught their teenagers important lessons about life: They are up to dealing with loss and crisis can be handled with care and dignity.

The next day the basketball team lost in a hotly contested championship game. Before the game there was a moment of silence for Coach Lennon, followed by words of praise for Coach Mignano, the assistant coaches, and Mike Schwenk. The entire basketball season seemed like an eternity. Undoubtedly, it was an incredible performance by skilled educators like Sal Mignano, Mike Schwenk, the assistant coaches, and leaders in the school community, who quietly and respectfully allowed their colleague to die in dignity, surrounded by their unwavering support. They allowed Cliff to make the decisions that were best for him and his students, and they resisted the urge to take his coach's mantle away.

Coaches like Cliff Lennon and Sal Mignano can be found in many of our schools, coaches who lift the spirits and hopes of students and also guide them through the personal crises that can emerge. Part of the definition of the word "coach" is being an "instructor." As we can see in this real story, that instruction is not just about teaching rebounding and fast break to student athletes. It is also about continuing on when adversity strikes and finding avenues of participation that work even in bad times.

- *School Support Staff.* School monitors, bus drivers, secretaries, security personnel, and so on are another valuable, but underused, source of informal data in the schools. These are the people who engage students in the cafeterias, detention rooms, and the assistant principal's office; at dances and athletic events; in the hallways; and on school grounds. Many support staff are neighbor parents and know a great deal about the family life of students. Conversely, they are known, along with their family life and stories, by the students, often being called by their first names. These are key adults who serve as both a beacon and antenna for the school, drawing students into intimate and personal conversations while at the same time being sensitive to changes in behavior that might signal trouble, as with Taylor Hooton, J. Daniel Scruggs, Melissa Smith, and the Mepham football players.

While they may lack formal training and degrees, many support staff members are street smart. Their daily interactions with students who are headed for trouble have provided them with fast-track training in how to observe, listen to, and guide students toward open doors of help. They hear the latest gossip about parents who are divorcing, an overdose at a party, a death in the family, and ongoing physical abuse of a young ninth grader by a senior athlete. They also connect with students headed for addiction, who routinely smoke cigarettes while cutting class.

Their advantage, and gift, as a premier source of informal data lies in the fact that they are not professional and carry no professional trappings when interacting with students. They realize that the hallways, cafeteria, and smoking areas on remote locations on the school grounds all belong to students. It is their territory. As such, these areas, all potential data-gathering venues, serve as arenas of comfort where students feel free to tell their stories and share their troubles, not only with peers but with easily accessible and trustworthy support staff, many of whom have raised children and have wisdom gained from real-life experience. One final advantage that support staff have in guiding marginal students is that they know the effective helpers in the school, the counselors, teachers, administrators, students, and community professionals who deliver when students need intervention.

Laurie R. is one of those highly qualified support staff members. The mother of five grown children, she has been a grounds monitor at Shoreham-Wading River High School for twenty years. Her children have all gone through the schools and she knows many families on an intimate basis. Her work as grounds monitor places her in daily contact with class cutters, smokers, and those students in retreat and hiding out. Her approach is simple with smokers: "Don't light up where I can see you or I'll have to turn you in. But what good would that do? Nurse Esper and Dr. Fibkins run a smoking group. It meets tomorrow during third period. If you're interested I'll speak to them and get you an invitation. Give me your homeroom teacher's name and I'll make sure there's a pass for you tomorrow morning. You've been talking about stopping smoking for the past month. Let's do it."

Laurie in a sense is the go-to person on the school grounds when students first consider changing acting-out and destructive behavior. She, like Lorraine Esper, can be confrontational and give students headed for the margins advice and suggestions they don't want to hear but know are right on target. Laurie is often the first stop for these students on their way for help. Is she without critics? No, there are professionals in the school who say that the helping process should be left to those people who are credentialed and have formal training.

They say Laurie and other support staff should do only what they are paid to do—catch the smokers, keep the bathrooms and stairwells free of cutters, and so on. They shouldn't be involved in personal interventions. Leave it to the professionals. What's missing in this response is that the few professionals in the school who deal with counseling can't do it all. To be effective, they need teachers, students like Kathy in her concern for Rob, coaches like Sal Mignano and Cliff Lennon, and support staff like Laurie to be first responders, deliver the invitation to help, when trouble arrives in the lives of students and their families. It takes a team effort that is shared by many members of the school community, a team in which each helping resource is respected and valued, regardless of their formal degrees, credentials, and professional status.

- *Parents*. Again, the beginning steps in helping marginal students be directed to reliable sources of help aren't rocket science. The process calls for the helping person to be known to students, trusted, and willing to be involved in a personal relationship that includes the opportunity to find an avenue, an open door, to change a troubling behavior and/or situation.

As I have suggested, it means helping students find an arena of comfort in the school, home, and within themselves. In this relationship simple words of caring and concern work best. It's a role that does not require a counseling degree but rather an interest in and dedication to wanting to be of help, backed up by a life experience of resolving problems. We all know the words that encourage us to tell our stories and ask for help. "How are you doing today?" "Tell me about that bruise on your arm. It looks painful." "What's going on with your parents' divorce?" "You seem upset about Rob's going into rehab." "How was your grandfather's funeral? I know you were very close to him." "What happened to Rob Pace was a tragedy. I know you were very close to him." "How are you doing? I know you are uneasy about going to Calvin Kohart's wake. Let's talk about what you think it might be like." We all know the words that tend to silence and send the troubled teen into retreat. "Time heals all wounds. Keep thinking positively." "Growing up is difficult. You have to learn to adjust to these things." "Maybe you should see a psychiatrist. I'm not trained to help you." "What you are saying makes me anxious. Maybe you should try harder to talk to your parents. I'm sure they're not as bad as you make them out to be." "I'm sure your father wouldn't have hit you unless you did something to provoke him."

There are many parents who can also fulfill the role of first responders to help neighborhood teens headed for trouble and in this role serve as beacons and antennae for the intervention system in the school. Maybe not for their own children, because there is too much of ourselves and our emotions involved in trying to help our own kids. But our helping gifts as concerned parents can be put to good use when we observe parents in the neighborhood struggling to cope with a son or daughter headed toward the margins. It could be something like this in the case of Judith Scruggs, knocking on her door, asking her to talk and in the conversation suggesting one small step forward out of her troubled life by saying, "Let's do one thing. Catholic Charities has a clinic in Bridgeport. It's fifteen minutes away. Let's drive over there and see if we can get you an appointment with a counselor. On the way back maybe we can stop at the school and try to get some answers on why Daniel is being abused every day. Get some answers and expect the school to do some intervention."

Another parent might talk with Rob's parents about his sudden hospitalization using such words as, "This must be very hard on you both, a shock, really. It was for me and the neighbors. But the good news is that he is getting the help he needs, before it got worse. How about the two of you? How are you coping with it all? Are you getting some counseling and support? Please know that I am here, across the street, and don't be a stranger and keep it all inside and to yourself."

In the case of Cliff Lennon an approach might be to knock on his door and say, "I noticed your car in the driveway lately and heard rumors about your being ill. I just wanted to stop by and see how you are doing. I also heard through the grapevine that you might need some meals made and some laundry and cleaning done. I'd like to help out. How are your sons doing with it all? I am involved with some of the support groups at St. Joseph's; I know you are parishioners there. Maybe Brian and Bill might want to come by. It could be of help to them. Let me know. Here's my phone number. I'll come by tomorrow. I'm cooking up some lasagna and will make a plate for you guys. Anything else you need?"

Again, an effective intervention team involves many different actors functioning on many different levels. Administrators, counselors, teachers, students, school nurses, support staff, parents, and community resources all have a significant role on this team. They are ready and set to respond to a troubled teen and his or her family, to share their observations, plan intervention strategies and act, as in the case of Cliff Lennon, which included a number of first responders such as his team members, principals, school nurse, counselors, coaches, and peer counselors.

- *Kids in Need (KIN) Committee.* What is missing in many of our schools is a central agency that is empowered to monitor each student headed toward the margins and is set to respond with an effective intervention strategy that can quickly spring into action. The agency must help the school shine the light on every student and foster a school-wide awareness that even the best and brightest can find themselves heading toward the margins given changing conditions in their home life, relationships, and health and well-being. The student taking three advanced placement courses can suddenly become the one cutting himself with a razor. The agency must serve as an outreach resource for students, staff, and parents in addition to the Child Study Team (CST) model now in place in our schools that focuses on the most seriously acting out, at-risk students, those with learning disabilities and handicapping conditions in need of special education and whose referral and data gathering process is often limited to these students.

What our students need in addition to the Child Study Team model is a Kids in Need Committee. This is a model I helped develop at Shoreham-Wading River High School in our effort to move our intervention focus from the narrow focus of addressing only at-risk students to including every student in the school. This committee was chaired by the principal and was made up of a team of school counselors, psychologist, social worker, teacher leader, and community mental/physical health resource. The charge of the committee is to meet once per week to review the student well-being profile data developed by the principal's office, the informal data that has come to the attention of KIN members, identify students who may need intervention, and formulate an intervention plan that includes the student's personal adult advocate, teachers, and parents or guardians. The members of KIN are also charged with responding to crises such as the accidental death or suicide of a student, parent, or staff member.

The KIN model I am proposing here moves beyond the model developed at Shoreham-Wading River in that it incorporates the formal data gathered from the student well-being profile and the informal data process identified earlier in the chapter. Picture this scene. In the KIN meeting room each member has access to a personal computer station that contains up-to-date information on each student. When members bring a referral and informal observation data to the meeting, they can quickly turn to the SWP data for trends and movements toward the margins, as in the case of J. Daniel Scruggs' truancy and Taylor Hooton's fights at school, acting out behavior, and changing physical appearance. In the cases of Rob Pace, Calvin Kohart, and Cliff Lennon, members can use the informal data observations they are hearing to develop intervention strategies to support students, staff, and parents who are dealing with death and loss. And in the case of Nick Adenhart, they can use the data to develop an intervention strategy responding to another kind of loss, the loss of a dream.

In a sense both the Child Study Team and the Kids in Need Committee complement each other and add to the smooth running of an effective intervention system. The Child Study Team, made up of the school psychologist, special education teachers, social worker, nurse, and counselors, many of whom are members of the Kids in Need Committee, focuses on interventions for students with learning disabilities, handicapping issues, and state/federal special education mandates and guidelines. The work of the Kids in Need Committee is focused on the entire student body by observing trends and movement toward the margins, offering a more expanded, school-wide vision of who needs intervention.

However, creating an agency such as the Kids in Need Committee to serve as a clearinghouse to monitor and identify students headed for trouble isn't enough in itself. All the data in the world is worthless if it is not used to develop a specific intervention plan that includes clear pathways of help, with open doors that signal an arena of comfort, open doors that are easily accessible and allow the intervention work to go on unfettered, hopefully to a successful conclusion.

The intervention plan should be very specific and identify the professionals involved and the plan they are following. Simply recommending that a student needs "counseling" is not enough. If "counseling" is recommended, what will be involved? Will it be one-on-one or in groups? Which counselor will lead the intervention? What other kinds of support will be offered to the student, such as the opportunity to be a peer counselor? What kinds of counseling support will be involved for the parents? What specific outreach will be made to community mental health and health agencies? What kinds of support and guidance will be offered to the student's teachers?

And there has to be one person, the student's personal adult advocate, who has been identified by the KIN committee as the go-to person to monitor and coordinate the progress of a student who has been referred by the committee and make sure all parties involved in the intervention process—teachers, counselors, and parents—are acting in support of the process and regularly report back to the KIN committee on progress or lack of same. Creating this kind of effective delivery system that can quickly respond to students headed toward the margins is a key element in a successful intervention system.

As University of Chicago sociologist Ronald S. Burt suggests, the value of a good idea is not in its origin but in its delivery.[33] All our efforts to develop a KIN Committee and utilize the data garnered from the student well-being profile and informal data sources will fall short if we are unwilling or unable to alter our present out-of-date intervention system and replace it with a variety of new open doors of help that make sense to today's students and parents. We need to move beyond the current limited intervention approach in most schools that, as researchers Virginia Richardson and Patricia Colfer suggest, waits until school-related problems occur and then identifies the student exhibiting such behavior as at risk.[34]

Chapter 3 will focus on a variety of open doors that can be created in the school by principals to ensure students and parents get the help they need in a timely and professional manner and that professionals, such as the personal adult advocate, teachers, and support staff get the guidance and support they need to be effective helpers.

NOTES

1. Roberta G. Simmons, and Dale A. Blyth, *Moving into Adolescence: The Impact of Puberty Changes and School Contact* (New York: Aldine De Gruyter, 1987), xxi, 304, 351–352.

2. Warren Torgerson, *Theory and Methods of Scaling* (New York: Wiley, 1958), 54.

3. Kenneth A. Sirotnik, "Equal Access to Quality in Public Schooling: Issues in the Assessment of Equity and Excellence," in *Access to Knowledge: An Agenda for Our Nation's Schools*, eds. John I. Goodlad and Pamela Keating (New York: College Entrance Board, 1990), 171.

4. National Association of Secondary School Principals (NASSP), *Executive Summary of Breaking Ranks 11: Strategies for Leading High School Reform* (Reston, Va.: NASSP, 2004), 1–6.

5. Ann Hulbert, "Are the Kids All Right?" *New York Times Magazine*, 11 April 2004, pp. 9–10 (6).

6. Margaret C. Wang, Maynard C. Reynolds, and Herbert J. Walberg, "Serving Students at the Margins," *Educational Leadership* 52(4) (December 1994–January 1995): 1–9.

7. Marianne D. Hurst, "Columbine High: Five Years Later," *Education Week*, 14 April 2004; www.edweek.org/ewstory.cfm?slug=31columbine.h23 (accessed 20 April 2004).

8. Margaret A. McKenna, "Columbine Leaves Many Lessons Behind," *Newsday*, 21 April 2004, p. 45 (A).

9. Peter Travers, "Elephant," rollingstone.com, 2003; www.rollingstone.com/reviews/movie/review.asp?mid=2047649 (accessed 16 March 2004).

10. Ryan Cormier, "School Sued over Teen's Suicide: Parents Fault Abandonment on Field Trip," *Newsday*, 21 July 2000 (accessed 16 March 2004 via Suffolk County, New York, Cooperative Library System).

11. Joshi Pradnya, "Riverhead Teenager's Suicide Prompts Law," *Newsday*, 13 July 2001 (accessed 16 March 2004 via Suffolk County, New York, Cooperative Library System).

12. Paul Vitello, "Schooled in Overlooking Trouble," *Newsday*, 14 March 2004, pp. 6, 45 (A).

13. Karla Schuster, "Keeping Pride Alive," *Newsday*, 26 October 2003, pp. 3, 16 (A).

14. Keiko Morris, and Karla Schuster, "Coaches on Defense," *Newsday*, 31 March, 2004, pp. 2–53, 59 (A).

15. Patrick Healy, "2 LI Coaches in Hazing Case Are Removed from Teaching," *New York Times*, 25 March 2004, p. 5 (B).

16. Keiko Morris, and Karla Schuster, "Appalled and Sickened," *Newsday*, 11 March 2004, pp. 2–3, 59 (A).

17. Steve Jacobson, "Mepham: Can Any Good Come of It?" *Newsday*, 18 January 2004, p. 31 (B).

18. Steve Jacobson, "Mepham Divided: Victims, Villains," *Newsday*, 26 October 2003, p. 35 (B).

19. Jere Longman, "An Athlete's Dangerous Experiments," *New York Times*, 26 November 2003, pp. 1, 4 (D).

20. Longman, "An Athlete's Dangerous Experiments."

21. Dan Steinberg, "When You Get a Good Kid . . . It's Sad," washingtonpost.com, 29 May 2004; www.washingtonpost.com/ac2/wp-dyn/A65517-2004May28?language=printer (accessed 30 May 2004).

22. Tomoeh Murakami Tse, "Recalling Boy's 'Zest for Life,'" *Newsday*, 8 October 2003, p. 30 (A).

23. Marc Santora, "Case Tries to Link a Mother to Her Boy's Suicide," *New York Times*, 27 September 2003, pp. 1, 6 (B).

24. Lisa Sanders, "Diagnosis," *New York Times Magazine*, 21 September 2003, p. 24 (6).

25. Robert L. Sinclair, and Ward J. Ghory, "Last Things First: Realizing Equality by Improving Conditions for Marginal Students," in *Access to Knowledge: An Agenda for Our Nation's Schools*, eds. John I. Goodlad and Pamela Keating (New York: College Entrance Board, 1990), 129–30, 132–33, 137.

26. Catherine Gewertz, "Trusting School Community Linked to Student Gains," *Education Week*, 16 October 2002; www.edweek.org/ew/ewstirt,cfn?slug=07trist.h22 (accessed 14 January 2004).

27. Carla Smith, "A Model of Leadership," principals.org, January 2004; www.nassp.org/publications/plpl_model_leadership_0104.cfm (accessed 13 January 2004).

28. Eliot Levin, "One Kid at a Time," *Educational Leadership 59*(7) (April 2002): 29–32.

29. Karen Rasmussen, "Healthy Students, Staff, and Communities," Association for Supervision and Curriculum Development (ASCD), *Curriculum Update*, Fall 1999; www.ascd.org/readingroom/cupdate/1999/1fall.html (accessed 7 April 2002).

30. William L. Fibkins, "Combating Student Tobacco Addiction in Secondary Schools," *National Association of Secondary School Principals (NASSP) Bulletin 77*(557) (December 1993): 51–59.

31. Carolyn Ahl, "Helping At-Risk Kids Get 'Teen Smart,'" minoritynurse .com, 27 January 2002; www.minoritynurse.com;features/undergraduate/01-27-02g .html (accessed 10 May 2004).

32. William L. Fibkins, "When a Beloved Teacher and Coach Dies," *National Association of Secondary School Principals (NASSP) Bulletin 82*(597) (July 1998): 88–93.

33. Michael, Erard, "Where to Get a Good Idea: Steal It Outside Your Group," *New York Times*, 22 May 2004; www.nytimes.com/2004/05/22/arts/22IDEA.html (accessed 28 May 2004).

34. Virginia Richardson, and Patricia Colfer, "Being At-Risk in School," in *Access to Knowledge: An Agenda for Our Nation's Schools*, eds. John I. Goodlad and Pamela Keating (New York: College Entrance Board, 1990), 111.

3

Creating an Effective Student Intervention System

As the *Breaking Ranks 11* report suggests, the idea for comprehensive change may not begin in the principal's office, but it most assuredly can end there, either through incomplete planning, failure to involve others, or neglect or failure to create conditions that allow a new order of things to emerge in the high school.[1] Creating these conditions is often the first challenge and sometimes it must start within the principal's own thinking and interaction with people. Key words here are "interaction with people." The principal of the school must be seen as a model for the helping process and stress personalization if an effective intervention system is to flourish. Therefore, a major part of the principal's role is to maintain a highly visible presence; lead by example; know each student by his or her first name so he or she feels connected to the school; be interested in students' aspirations and what they have to say; know what is going on in students' lives both inside and outside school; make the school a place of hope, trust, and respect; and as principal Doug Lowery Jr. suggests, take the time to help kids and make sure they are known, not just educated.[2]

They must create a climate and culture of personalization that encourages fellow administrators, counselors, teachers, support staff, students, and parents to buy into the vision that they, in their own unique way, are well positioned to offer help to students and parents headed for trouble, not turn a blind eye. They must use the position of the principal's office to continually remind all members of the school community that their intervention is critically important to maintaining a responsive schoolwide intervention climate. In this process the principal, as the head helper in the school, creates the expectation and awareness that every member of the school community counts as a potential source of help and discourages behaviors that lead to looking the other way when troubled students seek help. As a part of this process, he or she must provide the resources to train counselors, teachers, support staff, students, and parents as helpers.

As Margaret Wheatley, author of *Turning to One Another: Simple Conversations to Restore Hope for the Future*, advises, "Life always organizes as networks. Do you run your family, do you run your life, like an organization chart? It doesn't work. What works is realizing that for us to do our work well, we must be in relationships with lots of different people. We are interdependent. Pioneering species never forget that we are connected at the roots and that it's natural to be together."[3]

This approach to developing an effective intervention system does require some rethinking of the principal's role in reform. For example, Marge Scherer, editor of *Educational Leadership*, suggests that listening to constituents is a radical departure from the way we typically run schools. Although we may think we are listening, students and their families don't always agree. A recent Met Life survey notes that two-thirds of students believe that a principal must listen to students to be a good principal, but only one-fourth of principals agree that listening to students is of key importance. In addition, nine in ten principals say that their own school has open communication yet only six in ten teachers and parents agree.

Research by Pedro A. Noguera points out the need to listen to students when attempting to transform high schools into more personalized learning environments to counteract pervasive student alienation, boredom, strained relationships between adults and students, and anti-intellectual peer cultures that undermine efforts to raise academic achievement.[4] As important, this research recognizes the critical role of the principal in providing training and expecting school staff to successfully carry out this new aspect of their work. In a study of ten Boston, Massachusetts, high schools, he found that some schools just go through the motions, whereas other schools listen to teachers, parents, and students and make sure stakeholders understand the purpose of reform.

In his study, Noguera found that the schools' attempts to personalize school through an advisory system, in which teachers served as student counselors through an extended homeroom period held once a week, seemed effective. "We sat in on several advisory classes where no advising was occurring. The teachers obviously had no idea of how to use the allotted time and most lacked experience in counseling." Noguera also reports, "At all of the ten schools in the project we asked students, 'Is there an adult at your schools to whom you would turn if you were experiencing a serious personal problem?' With the exception of two of the schools more than 80 percent of the students at each school replied, 'No.' We also asked students if they believed their teachers were concerned about how well they did in school. Disturbingly, 56 percent of the students said they did not believe that their teachers really cared."

Noguera and Scherer's advice needs to be listened to by principals who are committed to reforming outdated intervention systems. The bottom line is that one can't bring about real reform without creating conditions that allow a new order of things to emerge. It is not enough, and in the long run is harmful to both teachers and students, to introduce a teacher-led advisory system in which the teachers lack training in counseling and have no idea how to use the allotted time and where no advising occurs. Yet, as Noguera suggests, many administrators continue to assume that changes in the organizational structure of schools will automatically result in a more personalized learning environment, that simply adopting a teacher-led advisory system (or as the *Breaking Ranks 11* report suggests, a personal adult advocate role for each student) will lead to more effective personal and academic intervention and fewer students heading toward the margins.

As sociologist Ronald S. Burt reminds us, the value of a good idea or changes in the organizational chart of an institution is not in its origin but in its delivery.[5] What we need to be about is making sure that changes in the organizational structure of the school are actually working to respond to students' personal and academic needs and we are delivering what has been promised on paper, not, as in the case of the Boston schools, where the creation of advisories became faux fronts, not real reform. That is an example of how promised reform becomes watered down and everyone in the school community loses. Teachers lose their professional self-worth and integrity because they are not trained in how to provide an open door of help that is required of an effective advisor.

Students who need personal and academic intervention lose faith in their school and teachers when they find the heralded open door of an advisory is just another closed door. Parents also lose faith in the promise of the public school when they find the advisory role of creating more personalized attention for their children has no substance to it. And principals themselves, who publicly tout these new organizational changes but in reality know teacher advisors are not delivering a more personalized learning environment, also lose faith in their own ability to bring about real reform. In the end, every member of the school community begins to understand that what is taking place is that they are pretending real change is occurring when in reality everyone—students, teachers, and administrators—is going through the motions.

The first step, then, in transforming our intervention systems begins with principals being clearly focused on envisioning the various parts of an effective system; communicating their vision to every segment of the school community, such as fellow administrators, counselors, social workers, school psychologists, teachers, support staff, students, and parents, and getting their feedback and commitment to the plan for change; providing training that serves as a vehicle for moving the various parts of the new intervention system from the idea to the reality stage; knowing how to overcome resistance to this new system; continually reassessing whether this system is meeting the ever-changing needs of students heading toward the margins; and knowing how to avoid being lulled into thinking that just because there has been a change in the school's organization chart, such as adding an advisory program or personal adult advocate model, that quality intervention will automatically follow. As sociologist Burt advises, potentially good ideas often die at the hands of those who brought them. Managers have a wide gap between coming up with good ideas and making them happen.

Principal Doug Lowery provides an excellent role model for this process. He understands that although he may be seen as a major role model for helping students, he can't do it alone. He can be a presence, be visible in the hallways, know every student by his or her first name, know students' aspirations, and create a safe haven in the school for students. But he also understands that in order to reach his goal of maintaining a high level of personalization, he needs all the parts of the school community— counselors, teachers, support staff, students, parents—on board and giving 100 percent to deliver on what has been promised to the students and parents. "I believe in the team concept," said Lowery. "We win together; we struggle together; we're all involved." His thoughts about a team concept are echoed by Jean Shackle, a seventh grade language arts teacher at Hilliard Memorial, who said of Lowery, "He makes sure he knows who you are, what your goals are, and gets people to work together for the common cause of education. He always comes up with ideas that will help us help the kids."

I am sure that Lowery and principals like him do not come to the role of a major source of help to students and parents without a great deal of introspection and the hard work involved in becoming more aware of and open to students and their problems, coming from different backgrounds and cultures. As Scherer reports, listening to constituents is a radical departure from the way we typically run schools, but it's the only way to build community.

Clearly Lowery had to develop an awareness of the kinds of students and parents he had difficulty relating to. No principal walks into a school and relates well to every student. And clearly he had to develop an awareness of the kinds of student problems he would choose to avoid if he felt they were "too hot to handle." He also had to become aware of those students whom he was more comfortable with and who came from a background and culture similar to his own. He had to be aware that he might tend to spend more time with those students to whom he is attracted and overlook others who were moving toward the margins.

Lowery probably had to resist peers who cautioned him that he needed to be in the office and handle the details of school life, not leave his office vacant and be out greeting students as they come off the buses, making thirty class visits a week, helping serve lunch, playing football with students during their lunch, and attending extracurricular events after school and on weekends. And he probably had to reeducate counselors and teachers who revisited playing a major role in helping students to resolve their personal problems before they reached the crisis stage. No doubt he had to educate support staff, students, and parents that they had to play a major role in intervening and referring students and parents heading toward the margins. As superintendent Dale McVey reports, "Doug has a broad knowledge base but strives to expand upon that each year."

Our task has many parallels to Lowery's work. In creating a new intervention system, we need to clearly articulate how the various parts of an effective intervention operate and complement each other so that, as Lowery suggests, "We are all involved," that each part has a major role to play in the intervention scheme and are interdependent and connected. It is a process that builds on Wheatley's notion that for educators to do our work, we must be in relationships with a lot of different people, each of whom, whether they are administrators, counselors, teachers, support staff, students, or parents, has a role to play in helping students headed toward the margins. It is the process of involving these various members of the schoolwide intervention response team that enables principals like Doug Lowery to create the conditions necessary for other members of the school community to participate and share in the responsibility for responding to troubled students, to communicate that he, as principal, can't be the only model of an open door for help and that their contributions are expected and needed.

Here is a vision of how principals can build the various parts of an up-to-date intervention system that will allow a new order of things to emerge, an order in which counselors, school nurses, teachers as personal adult advocates, support staff, students, and parents team together to provide a safe haven for each student.

REORGANIZING THE GUIDANCE AND COUNSELING SERVICES

The guidance and counseling services represent the flagship piece of the intervention system I am calling for, a system that offers easily available and accessible individual and group counseling opportunities as well as training for teachers as personal student advocates, support staff as helpers, students as peer helpers and leaders, and parents as outreach helpers for parents headed toward trouble. It is a system that includes counselor colleagues who are effective in meeting the demands of the school organization for scheduling students, testing, college advisement, and career counseling. In a sense, the initial labeling of guidance programs as "guidance *and* counseling" was right on target, offering legitimacy and respect to both the guidance/information advising and counseling role of counselors, equal partners in helping each student become all he or she can be.

However, in my experience in working to transform guidance and counseling services to include personal counseling for students and parents, the first wave of resistance to change often comes from counselors themselves. This should be expected and come as no surprise to reform-minded principals and counselor leaders. As education historian Robert Hampel has described, the history of the school guidance and counseling movement clearly demonstrates that when counselors are faced with carrying out the demands of the school organization, they give high priority to the college selection process, testing, and assigning students to classes.[6]

They more often than not assign a lower priority to intervening to offer counseling to students headed toward the margins. But reform-minded principals and counselor leaders need to avoid blaming the counselors for this situation. Beginning an effort to successfully bring about change doesn't get far with blame. In a real sense this situation has been forced on them. Giving less attention to offering individual and group counseling to troubled students is not their fault nor should they be blamed for this process. Counselors are merely following the script that has been written for them. While the 1964 American School Counseling Association (ASCA) *Statement of Policy for Secondary School Counselors* heralded a new era in which counselors would give high priority to counseling students on personal issues, those results are hard to find in today's secondary schools.

Here are some of the goals in the ASCA statement of policy. "The role of the school counselor is concerned with and accepts responsibility for assisting all pupils, having as his [or her] major concern the developmental needs and problems of youth. [Counselors] see counseling as a dynamic relationship between counselor and counselee and cite the counselor's responsibility of becoming involved with pupils and their behaviors. The counselor's focus is on growth and development of pupils and on helping pupils to enhance and enrich their personal development and self-fulfillment by means of making more intelligent decisions."[7]

But as Hampel (1986) points out, the guidance departments that emerged in the mid-1960s never analyzed teenagers' emotions to the extent envisioned by reformers. They were greeted as quasi-administrators whose main priority was to help students with course selection and advise them on college placement. As Hampel reports, counselors became the mediators between students and the school bureaucracy with a physical and symbolic location closer to the administration. Authors Arthur G. Powell, Eleanor Farrar, and David Cohen support Hampel's view of a guidance system in which counselors serve as quasi-administrators who often do not provide an open door for troubled students.[8] They report that the advising received by most students is determined by the logistics of scheduling and meeting graduation requirements. "It's like you don't even know your counselor," one teenager complained. "You see him at the beginning of the year and that's it. You might as well not be here as far as he is concerned."

"You see a counselor once," another reported. "'You doing okay?' and I say, 'okay.'" One girl regarded her counselor as a kind of traffic cop who told her when to go and when to stop, which roads were open and which were blocked. "If I had a problem he'd be the last one I would go to." The reason she gave was, "He doesn't know me. He wouldn't be able to help."

Counselor educator David R. Cook suggests that counselors emerged as one of the main functionaries in implementing the sorting of students into classes, higher education and careers.[9] Cook also wisely observed that many counselors who might be adequate to the task of therapeutic counseling found that the demands of the school situation made it difficult, if not impossible, to carry out this kind of counseling. What evolved was a system in which both students and their counselors lost out on a more personalized relationship. The students lost out on a relationship in which they could be known by their counselors and receive the intervention they needed rather than viewing their counselor as the last one they would turn to for help.

Counselors trained in one-on-one and group intervention lost out as well. They were left with little or no opportunity to use their skills to help marginal students and their parents. They were told instead to put those personal counseling skills away for another day. For both students and counselors, there was the realization that personal problems of students headed toward the margins didn't really matter in the big picture of school life. One can argue that they turned a blind eye on the nonacademic side of students' lives. It wasn't a priority to take a closer look that might get at the problem that no one else at school or at home is noticing. Those counselors who did venture to look closely at troubled students were often looked upon as out of step, saviors, not fitting into the quasi-administrator role that was, and is, in vogue.

However, as the growing personal and nonacademic needs of students and parents emerged in the latter part of the twentieth century, counselors, as Cook suggests, found themselves trapped in an identity crisis, struggling with the question, "What is our role?" Cook suggests that the professionalization of school counseling has become something of a box in which the school counselor is trapped. The counselor has been seduced into functioning on behalf of the bureaucratic structure of the school. Despite a mountain of rhetoric about meeting "the needs of pupils," the reality is that it was the increasing bureaucratization of our school system that created the demands for the guidance services.

Reform-minded principals need to make the case to counselors that they, too, are caught in a box when it comes to putting into practice the recommendations of *Breaking Ranks 11.* How can they proceed to mount a schoolwide effort to know the aspirations, strengths, and weaknesses of each student and interact with "difficult" parents within a guidance and counseling service that is unable or unwilling to be proactive in knowing each student well and intervening when trouble arrives whether it be academic, personal, or health-related? The recommendations of *Breaking Ranks 11* cannot succeed without harnessing the long dormant training skills of counselors in order to provide training for faculty members who can serve as personal adult advocates, and students, support staff, and parents who can serve as critical sources of advice and referral on the front lines of the school.

Therefore, the school principal, as the lead helper in the school, needs to envision a new organizational framework and counselor roles for the guidance services in which well-trained counselors are assigned to offer individual and a variety of group counseling interventions for students headed toward the margins while other counselors attend to the business aspect of school such as scheduling, testing, admission to higher education, and vocational choices. This process would enable guidance staff to escape the professional box that has been created for them and return to their earlier professional vision offering both personal counseling and guidance services to students while enabling the principal to address the growing personal needs of marginal students and their parents unhindered by an out-of-date intervention system.

The following is a step-by-step road map on how principals can win over their guidance staff and begin the process of creating an effective intervention system.

1. Educate counselors to be aware that they are trapped, as Cook suggests, in a system that is growing more irrelevant each day as the

personal needs of students continue to increase and more attention is being paid to how personal and well-being problems serve to block academic success. In many schools, counselors have developed a "circle the wagons" mentality as they endure increased criticism of their inability to help troubled students—from teachers, students, and parents. They need to use their principal's bully pulpit to sell counselors on the pressing need to consider alternatives that will help to reinvent guidance services, raise their lagging morale, and connect them with new roles that offer the potential for professional growth and success. However, the reform-minded principals and counselors need to remind themselves constantly that there is tremendous pressure from colleges and universities to keep counselors in the role of quasi-administrators and college admission experts and relegate personal counseling to a minor or even nonexistent role, a "nice if we could offer kids more personal counseling but who has time" role.

The reality is that many members of the higher education community see guidance counselors as their ticket to maintaining their student enrollment and are increasing their wooing approach. Intentionally or not, college admissions directors want guidance counselors focused on guiding students into their colleges, not spending time solving personal problems. And they continuously work at shoring up this image of the counselor's role with perks.

Staff writer Gregg Winter describes the wooing process used by college admissions directors such as Victor I. Davolt of Regis University, located in Denver, Colorado.[10] Winter reports that for the past two years Davolt has been playing host to school guidance counselors, the "extremely influential" people he hopes will send more students to his ninety-acre campus. He flies them in from around the country to meet the faculty and review the curriculum. But he also includes skiing on the world-famous slopes of Vail, snowmobiling and spending time at a spa, and getting a facial or massage, all courtesy of the university. Davolt also treats counselors to professional hockey games and rooms at luxury hotels. Winter observes that although the image of the admissions process is often one of high school counselors sidling up to colleges in hopes of gaining an advantage for their students, the reality is sometimes the other way around.

Colleges are so intent on getting not just enough applicants, but the best ones, that some are lavishing perks on guidance counselors. For example, when the admissions staff at Center City College in Danville, Kentucky, invites guidance counselors to visit, it puts them up in a bed and breakfast and takes them golfing at a country club and to a racetrack. It even gives them a small stake, around fifty dollars, so they can gamble on the horses. Goucher College in Towson, Maryland, takes visiting counselors to the theater, the symphony, and Baltimore Orioles games and rents out the Rock and Roll Hall of Fame and museum for a night to thank counselors. Ralph S. Figueroa, director of college guidance at Albuquerque Academy, a private school in New Mexico, suggests, "We can't help but be swayed by the people who are nice to us, who buy nice things for us." These college excursions offer short-term but tangible rewards for guidance counselors in that they provide an open door through which they can escape from their often hectic school life, that can include dealing with critics, and instead be wined and dined and made to feel they are needed. Principals and counselor reformers need to be mindful of these powerful pressures when they begin asking counselors to redefine their services.

2. Encourage counselors to reject the response that what is needed is the hiring of more counselors to meet the growing personal needs of students. As education reporter Shelly Reese suggests, many counselors don't want new methods, they want more assistance.[11] The problem with this kind of response is that it is based on the notion of expanding resources in a time of increasingly limited resources for schools rather than on an examination of how to use the existing counseling resources to meet current needs. This response also overlooks the notion that hiring more counselors usually results in more resources being poured into the scheduling and testing aspect of counselors' work, not a shift to more individual and group counseling intervention. In my experience, in reforming schools the quasi-administrator role of the counselor is difficult, if not impossible, to change simply by adding new personnel to do "more of the same."

3. Focus counselors on ways to modernize their intervention system. To begin with, educate counselors to consider alternatives to the practice of simply assigning counselors to students by grade or alphabet

rather than counseling skills. Here is an example of this inefficient use of some well-trained counselors whose resources would be better utilized in leading intervention efforts for marginal students. The website of the guidance program at Sachem North High School in Lake Ronkonkoma, a grade 11 and 12 high school, indicates, "Counselors are assigned to a case load of students on an alphabetical basis."[12] These "Alpha Student Assignments" are made with such breakdowns as A-Bra, Bre-De, Di-Dy, E-G, and so on. Therefore if you are Nick Adenhart, Taylor Hooten, Rob Pace, J. Daniel Scruggs, or any student heading for the margins, your choice for counselor depends on the luck of the draw.

If you are fortunate, you may get a counselor who is well-trained in individual and group intervention. But if the luck of the draw doesn't go your way, you may end up with a counselor who, as students mentioned earlier reported, you see once a year, doesn't know your name, and would be the last person you would seek out for help and advice. Clearly students should not have to depend on the luck of the draw when troubles come their way. And well-trained counselors who can offer personalized counseling should not be herded into alpha and grade assignments in which their skills are used by only a few students whose names begin with A-Bra.

This organizational arrangement leaves much to be desired, leaving many students without an open door that can respond to their needs. While the American School Counselors Association National Model, *A Framework for School Counseling Programs*, calls upon schools to "ensure that every student has equitable access to the school counseling program," the assignment of counselors by alphabet or grade is in many ways not equitable, fair, or just for marginal students or their parents.[13]

The work of the principals then is to begin reshaping the guidance service by introducing and selling a plan to assign counselors by skills and talents. This might mean identifying a cadre of counselors who are trained, or can be trained, to offer one-on-one counseling, a variety of group interventions, and training for staff, students, and parents as helpers, as well as a cadre of counselors to carry out the guidance tasks such as scheduling, testing, and advice on admission to higher education or careers. In the process the principal must use his bully pulpit to publicly acknowledge that both counseling roles are important and valued.

4. Help counselors to rethink how to transform their services by providing a concrete example of a state-of-the-art guidance and counseling service. The following is my suggestion for such a program.

   a. Group counseling to help students deal with:
      - Development issues such as peer pressure and academic performance
      - Problems related to alcohol, tobacco, and drug abuse
      - Physical and/or sexual abuse issues
      - Diversity, for example, race, ability, and social

   b. Individual counseling to help:
      - Marginal students
      - Problems of gifted students

   c. Parent counseling groups focusing on:
      - Adolescent development
      - Parenting the marginal student
      - Parenting a gifted child
      - Parents who are marginal or at risk

   d. Training of teachers to be helpers/advisers to:
      - Identify/refer a troubled student
      - Hold effective parent–teacher conferences

   e. Training students and staff members to:
      - Help and/or refer students who are headed for the margins

   f. Pathways to rehab and reentry to school that include:
      - Mandatory individual counseling
      - Rehab for students who abuse alcohol or drugs or who have health-related problems
      - Reentry into school after rehab

   g. The Child Study Team (CST) and Kids in Need (KIN) Committee
      - CST is made up of leadership personnel in the school, for example, administrator, counselor, school psychologist, school nurse, teacher leaders. The CST meets to identify students with handicapping and learning conditions and initiate intervention.
      - KIN is also made up of members of the leadership team of the school along with the personal adult advocate of the student

being considered. The mission of KIN is to provide intervention for marginal students.

h. Individual counseling for higher education, vocation, and course
selection:
  • Individual counseling sessions available for students and parents
  to facilitate choice of higher education and academic course selection.

5. In discussing the various elements in a state-of-the-art guidance and
counseling service, focus counselors on the specifics of how, when,
and where they will respond to students headed toward the margin,
not using the vague words and approaches offered in the American
School Counselors Association's *National Model for School Counseling* developed in 2002.[14] In my opinion the model clings to the
outdated and vague role definitions of counseling such as "the
school counselor serves as change agent, collaborator, and advocate.
Through collaboration with other professionals in the school building, school counselors influence systemic change and advocate for
students by using strong communication, consultation, and leadership skills."

The report also inadvertently crystallizes the problems afflicting
the school counseling profession by stating, "The school mission of
2002 is not altogether different than in the 1960s. Today, in a world
enriched by diversity and technology, school counselors' chief mission is still supporting the academic achievement of all students so
they are prepared for the ever-changing world of the 21st century."[15]
The report also states, "Counselors trained in programs rooted in
psychological and clinical paradigms differed greatly from those
rooted in education paradigms. These changes and varying perspectives confused and caused role confusion among school counselors,
school administrators, teachers, parents, and guardians." In my view
there appears to be no recognition that the school's mission has
changed dramatically from the 1960s and now includes addressing
the personal and well-being needs of students as a way to increase
academic achievement, the need to envision new approaches to
guidance services to address these nonacademic needs, and an
awareness that many secondary school guidance departments are
experiencing staff cuts and staff attrition and the personal counsel-

ing aspect of their role is outsourced to part-time student assistance counselors and community social service agencies because school counselors have been unable to deliver on their promise to provide personal counseling for all students.

Counselors who are in the school only on a limited basis and, in fact, may not possess the one-on-one and group counseling skills of the school's full-time counselors now are deployed only as advisors on scheduling and testing. These full-time counselors may be trained in the psychological and clinical paradigm but are given little opportunity to do the important work of offering personal counseling. I believe a more accurate reading of the "role confusion among school counselors, school administrators, teachers and parents" suggests that as early as the 1960s, the need to offer personal counseling to students by well-trained and available personal counselors was blindsided by school administrators, teachers, parents, and some counselors themselves who refused to acknowledge that a personal counseling role was much needed and deserved to be a legitimate partner with the counselors' role of testing and scheduling.

Now, in a world where the pressing personal needs of students to be heard and known, the limiting box created for and by counselors, and the ongoing decision to maintain this box and ways of doing business, is coming home to roost. Retired Major General Robert E. Wagner, a special assistant to the president of Norfolk, Virginia State University, when speaking of the guidance services in the Norfolk public schools, suggests, "I don't think a lot of local counselors in Norfolk care about youngsters."[16] However, the executive summary of the ASCA national model, *A Framework for School Counseling Programs*, does offer a glimpse of possible changes in the way counseling programs are organized and perhaps new roles for counselors aimed at meeting the growing personal needs of students and parents.

The ASCA model suggests:

Comprehensive school guidance should free counselors to do what they do best and what only they can do. Most school counselors have a master's degree and are typically the only people in a school with formal training in both mental health and education. Although school counselors are team players who understand fair-share responsibilities within a school, they cannot be fully effective when they are taken away from essential counseling tasks to perform non-counseling activities such as building the master schedule, serving as testing coordinators, handling discipline, and carrying out clerical duties. Certain non-counseling duties should be eliminated or reassigned, if possible, so school counselors can use their skills and knowledge to focus on students' needs.

Remarks by former Secretary of Education Richard Riley also suggest a new awareness of the need for more personal involvement with students.[17] He suggests that high schools should provide more mental health counseling, allow students to keep the same counselor for four years, and turn homeroom periods into student advisory periods where students can discuss events relevant to their lives.

The major argument of the principals and counselors interested in reform is quite simple. The only way for counselors to compete in today's complex world is to offer very clear open doors for personal one-on-one and group counseling. It is not enough for the ASCA national model to suggest eliminating noncounseling tasks "if possible." There is a rising voice and demand from students, parents, and teachers for an effective guidance intervention system. Time is running out for counselors and students waiting for what is "possible" while they are still in a box, mired in a quasi-administrator and bureaucratic role.

The only road out of this box is for counselors, with the leadership, support, and prodding of the school's principal, to reexamine their role and current delivery system in light of the changing needs of students. As we all know, change is difficult. Counselors, whose entire careers have been spent in one system, even if the system is not working for them or their troubled students, find it difficult to restructure and develop intervention programs that work. We all tend to go with what we know, what we feel comfortable with, even if we are in a failing system. We do what we know.

Counselors are not malcontents. Rather, they simply do not know how to proceed to plan new approaches while mired in the trappings of an ineffective system. In a sense they are not different from their marginal students and their parents, who find themselves stuck in situations where they too need new skills and approaches.

The burning question for counselors is no longer, "Is it fair that we be asked to help students to solve both their academic and personal and well-being problems, given the demands of our job for scheduling, testing, college admissions, and so on?" In my experience clients such as students, parents, and teachers no longer want to hear excuses or whining about counselors being overworked. They want the job done. They want counselors who know them on a personal level, have an open door, have the skills to offer quick intervention, and provide a positive connection with their teachers and parents.

Is this current situation fair to counselors who have dedicated their professional lives to helping students? Probably not. But the question is not about fairness. We have gone beyond that point. Counselors can continue to argue the fairness question and throw up roadblocks but what is needed to quiet the debate about what they should be doing to help kids and their own effectiveness is action. Otherwise they are in a no-win and demoralizing situation. They need action plans to demonstrate that they are up to meeting the new needs of students. Therefore, the question counselors need to be asking is, "How do we programmatically address the growing personal needs of today's students and continue to meet the scheduling, testing, college admissions, and career planning aspects of our work?"

6. Once the principal has engaged counselors in a dialogue about transforming their services, provided a concrete example of a state-of-the-art guidance and counseling program, and made his argument for the need for change, the next step is to help counselors assess in clear terms what additional services need attention, given the needs of today's students and parents. I've found in my own work to help counselors reorganize their delivery system that a useful place to begin is for the counseling staff to complete my restructuring guidance services inventory (RGSI). I believe the RGSI is a useful starting point because it helps counselors focus on the following major issues in restructuring and reenergizing their guidance services.

What obstacles and areas of resistance can counselors expect in the change process? What personal and professional skill and level of commitment do counselors need if they expect to change their present delivery system? This proves reform-minded principals and counselor leaders need to remind counselors that while they can pray for potatoes, they also must be willing to pick up a hoe. That is, to act.

The action that is required is for counselors to consider their skills and present situation and then outline steps to bring about changes in the guidance services. The RGSI, then, is the vehicle that principals and counselor leaders can utilize to help counselors think out of the box, develop a new awareness, and consider viable options to the present way of delivering guidance services and allocating resources. The data garnered from the RGSI provides a way to begin the conversation about the changes that need to be made. In that sense the RGSI is not a scientific instrument but a way to assess the ways counselors view the program elements in a state-of-the-art guidance and counseling program and how they measure up, and to begin identifying which areas need more attention, for example, group counseling. Here is how the RGSI works to provide a way for counselors to pick up the hoe:

Restructuring Guidance Services Inventory

The Elements of a Successful Guidance Delivery System

Please rate your assessment of where you are in this program area by circling a number from 1 to 5 (1 being the highest and 5 being the lowest) on the scale opposite the program area.

Group Counseling

1. Groups to help students deal with development issues such as peer pressure, family problems, self-esteem, academic performance	1	2	3	4	5
2. Groups to help students deal with problems related to alcohol, tobacco, or drug abuse	1	2	3	4	5
3. Groups to help students deal with health-related problems, such as eating disorders	1	2	3	4	5
4. Groups to help students deal with family, physical, and/or sexual abuse	1	2	3	4	5
5. Groups to help students understand and respect the differences in each other (color, race, culture, ability, social, economic, and neighborhood)	1	2	3	4	5

Individual Counseling

1. Individual counseling sessions available for marginal students	1	2	3	4	5

2. Individual counseling sessions available for particular problems of gifted students, athletes, and musicians   1   2   3   4   5
3. Individual counseling sessions available for "the average kid" who makes no waves (people think these kids are fine so no one ever asks how they are doing)   1   2   3   4   5

Parent Counseling
1. Parent groups that focus on adolescent development   1   2   3   4   5
2. Parent groups that focus on parenting the marginal student   1   2   3   4   5
3. Parent groups that focus on parenting a gifted child   1   2   3   4   5
4. Individual counseling for parents who are marginal or have a child who is marginal   1   2   3   4   5

Training Administrators to be Models of the Helping Process
1. Training administrators to be a model of the helping process in their schools, for example, at faculty meetings, assemblies, and public events   1   2   3   4   5
2. Training administrators to incorporate teacher helping skills and ability to help students with personal problems into the supervision and teacher evaluation program   1   2   3   4   5

Training Teachers to be Helpers
1. Training teachers to be effective advisors and helpers for students with personal problems   1   2   3   4   5
2. Training teachers where and how to refer a troubled student   1   2   3   4   5
3. Training teachers to be aware of avoiding or being fearful of some students. What are the avoidance issues? Are they related to color, race, appearance, background, or ability?   1   2   3   4   5
4. Training teachers to be aware of spending too much time with some students at the expense of others.   1   2   3   4   5
5. Training teachers how to hold helpful parent–teacher conferences that encourage parents to seek help with personal issues for themselves and their children   1   2   3   4   5
6. Counselors serving as an ongoing resource and mentors for teachers as they become involved in the helping process   1   2   3   4   5

Training Students to be Peer Helpers
1. Ongoing training for students in how to intervene, help, and/or refer fellow students who are headed toward the margins   1   2   3   4   5
2. Counselors providing ongoing supervision for student peer helpers   1   2   3   4   5

(*continued*)

Training Support Staff to be Helpers
1. Ongoing training for support staff (monitors, aides, secretaries, and custodians) on how to intervene, help, and/or refer students who are headed toward the margins   1   2   3   4   5
2. Counselors serving as an ongoing resource and mentors for support staff as the become involved in the helping process   1   2   3   4   5

Training Parents to be Helpers
1. Ongoing training for parents on how to intervene, help, and/or refer students and parents headed toward the margins   1   2   3   4   5
2. Counselors serving as an ongoing resource and mentors for parents as they become involved in the helping process   1   2   3   4   5

Creating Pathways to Rehab and Reentry into School
1. Mandatory individual counseling, in lieu of suspension, for students who abuse alcohol and/or drugs at school activities   1   2   3   4   5
2. Clear pathways to rehab for students who require rehabilitation for alcohol or drug abuse and health-related problems, such as eating disorders. Mechanism is in place to provide ongoing school and peer/faculty/parent support while in rehab   1   2   3   4   5
3. Clear pathways for reentry into school after rehab. Mechanism is in place to provide ongoing school and community support   1   2   3   4   5

Coordinating Resources for Referral in the Community
1. Counselor is the "point person" to identify referral sources in the community   1   2   3   4   5
2. Counselor provides training for faculty, support staff, administrators, and peer helpers on when, where, and how to refer   1   2   3   4   5

Leadership Role on Child Study Team and Kids in Need Committee
1. CST and KIN are made up of leadership personnel in the school, for example, administrator, counselor, school psychologist, school nurse, and teacher leaders. KIN identifies marginal students with handicapping and learning conditions   1   2   3   4   5

Individual Counseling for Higher Education, Vocation, and Course Selection
1. Individual counseling sessions available for students and parents to facilitate choice of higher education institution, financial planning, and academic course selection   1   2   3   4   5

In a perfect world the above-described program elements would be in place and running smoothly. In fact, many schools *do not have these elements in place.* These program elements are doable and attainable. But in the real world in which we live, many of us have only a few of the program elements in place. We have a vision and are willing to work hard to attain a state-of-the-art guidance program but we are not skilled in the change process and the politics of change. We try but we get stuck as we attempt to move our guidance programs into the twenty-first century. In the next section, let's take a look at how you, as a counselor leader, deal with the change process. Remember, good ideas and good intentions are no good without knowledge and real life experience in the change process.

Skills Needed to Implement a New Guidance Delivery System

Here are some important skills counselors need to know about the change process if they are going to implement a new guidance delivery system. How do you rate yourself?

1. I am able to accurately assess the personal needs of students in my school — 1 2 3 4 5
2. I am able to envision intervention programs that will meet the needs of these students — 1 2 3 4 5
3. I am able to understand the political dynamics in my school. I know which administrators, teachers, parents, and citizens have power — 1 2 3 4 5
4. I am able to sell those in power on a step-by-step plan to increase the effectiveness of our guidance program — 1 2 3 4 5
5. I am able to get my fellow counselors on board the program — 1 2 3 4 5
6. I have good public relations and marketing skills. I know how to sell this product — 1 2 3 4 5
7. I am in excellent physical and mental shape and can withstand the mental and physical cost involved in a change process — 1 2 3 4 5
8. I can take the "hit" of criticism, personal and professional, that comes with a change process — 1 2 3 4 5
9. I have a good professional and personal support network in place that I can turn to — 1 2 3 4 5
10. I have a wholesome personal life and family relationships that will help support me in the crunch — 1 2 3 4 5

(continued)

---

11. As a counselor leader I know how to take care of
my daily business so that I don't become a target
for criticism   1   2   3   4   5

Describe yourself, your present job situation, and some small steps you can
take to begin the road toward a restructuring of your guidance program.

Describe your professional skills and tell why you might be considered a
"counselor leader" and a "leader for change."

Describe your present job situation, illuminating the "pluses" and "minuses"
of the job.

List some small steps you can take to begin changing your guidance program.

The data gathered from the RGSI sets the stage for conversations about change, such as which counselors can take the lead in offering personalized one-on-one and group counseling; in advising administrators on how to model the helping process; in training teachers as personal adult advocates and advisors; in training students, support staff, and parents as helpers; in creating pathways to rehab and reentry to school; in coordinating resources for referral to community; in counseling students with special education needs; in playing a leadership role in CST and KIN Committee; and which counselors will take the lead in offering guidance information and advice such as scheduling, testing, college placement, and career choice.

7. The principal needs to keep in mind that the process of successfully transforming guidance and counseling services needs to go beyond the programmatic data gathered from the RGSI and include a personal component that helps counselors focus on their helping philosophy, skills, and attitudes toward the helping process. For example, the principal needs to encourage the counseling staff to begin a

process of assessing their strengths and weaknesses as helpers to students, whether it be in the personal counseling or guidance advising realm, and institute an ongoing training curriculum in order to keep their counseling skills at a high level. This training program can be led by counselors and members of the school's helping team, such as school psychologist, school nurse, social worker, community medical and mental health personnel, and in some cases, the principal and some skilled teachers.

How does the principal begin the process of helping counselors become aware of their own need for professional growth and training that is ongoing and centered in their school? Counselor leaders can develop this kind of a training curriculum by using my counselor self-awareness inventory. This inventory provides counselors with a way to focus on their own unique journey into the counseling profession and what gifts and opportunities they bring to their student, parent, and staff clients, as well as the walls and roadblocks they tend to put up to avoid some student, parent, and staff clients.

For example, what events or influences led them to want to help others? Could it be that they were marginal students as teens, headed for trouble? Who were/are their models in the helping process? Was there a counselor, teacher, coach, school nurse, peer, school secretary, or neighborhood parent who intervened to offer help, guidance, and support? What personal goals do they aspire to in helping others? Is it possible that they are giving back the help they received as teens to students troubled in the same way? What fears and concerns do they have about helping others, such as fear of failure? It is not easy helping others; the process includes many failed attempts until one overture finally works. What kinds of students do they tend to avoid? What kinds of students do they tend to gravitate toward? What kinds of student problems do they tend to stay clear of? What kinds of student problems do they feel free to embrace?

All counselors arrive at their desks with personal histories that make it easy to include like-minded students and problems that they have dealt with along the way and difficult to include different students and problems that cause anxiety, distancing, and quick referral to others. What are their strengths as helpers? Are they good listeners, empathetic, able to confront, be nonjudgmental? What are the helping skills that need improvement? Are they quick to give advice, reluctant to tackle real-life issues of students, such as suicide, death of a parent, and so on? Do counselors have a professional/ personal support group they can turn to for advice and support? When problematic issues arise can they call on family members, colleagues, and friends for honest feedback or are they on their own? In my experience, completing the inventory can often reveal critical insights into the issues and concerns counselors are struggling with when they offer to help students, issues that once brought out into the open can be used as the cornerstone for an ongoing training curriculum. Here are some examples of counselor concerns:

- I feel I don't know how to step away as a helper. I tend to carry student problems home and agonize over how I should respond. I'd like to share more of my concerns with my family and colleagues but no one seems interested. They think I am a very good counselor and don't really know what is going on inside me.
- I sometimes feel I miss important signs from some of my students who are asking for help.
- I don't know if I am a good counselor or just average. I haven't had anyone observe my counseling skills since graduation and that's ten years past.
- I've tried setting up counseling groups by posting notices on bulletin boards and telling teachers but no one ever shows up.
- I tend to give quick answers and advice and not listen to my students' worries.
- Student problems like suicide and abuse stir up a lot of anxiety in me and make me feel I can't handle these high-emotion problems well.
- I lack confrontation skills that are sometimes needed with students, parents, and teachers. My personality is a quiet one and I tend to avoid conflict.
- I definitely have trouble counseling students who are homosexual — gay or lesbian. Those kids make me feel so uncomfortable.
- I get too emotionally involved with my students. I don't see the line between being a professional and being a friend or parent surrogate with my students. It's not good.

- I am too sensitive and a bit judgmental. The judgments really bother me, as I know I am not supposed to respond that way.
- I don't have a clue about leading groups. I had no group training in grad school. Now I hesitate to start groups because I feel I won't know how to handle students in a group situation.
- I have a hard time accepting and helping students who appear lazy and not willing to put in the hard work needed to be successful.
- I feel that some students think I am too old to know how they feel.
- I worry about saying something or not saying something that will hurt, even damage, one of my students.
- My questioning skills stink. I get lost in my own thoughts and jumble my words.
- I find myself leaning toward students who are victims and underdogs and avoiding the high achievers. I was one of those underdog kids as a teen and I relate better to them. But is it fair to my high achievers who get less attention?
- I'd like to learn how to hide my anxiety when a powerful emotional issue comes up with my students, such as a sudden death of a parent or a brutal divorce.
- I have trouble helping students who are mean and push other kids around. My professional self knows they need help and insight about their behavior but personally I want to yell at them.

These kinds of concerns from counselors provide meaningful material for planning a training curriculum to improve counselors' one-on-one and group counseling skills. Each of the counselors' responses listed earlier can be used as a training workshop theme. Here is a possible fifteen-session training workshop to better prepare staff to be more effective counselors that culminates with counselors practicing one-on-one and group counseling roles using fellow counselors role-playing real student issues:

a. Identify and learn how to counsel students who threaten us and make us feel uncomfortable
b. Identify and learn how to counsel students whose problems threaten us and make us feel uncomfortable
c. Learn how to listen to all your students, not a select few

d.   Learn how to ask open-ended questions

e.   How do you—students, teachers, parents—perceive your counseling skills?

f.   How to persist in the helping process when your students are in denial and resist your well-intentioned efforts

g.   How to assess your judgmental level and become more inclusive

h.   How to keep a professional distance between you and needy students. Avoid falling into the trap of becoming a friend or even surrogate parent

i.   How to confront students, teachers, and parents who are headed toward trouble and need honest, even harsh, feedback

j.   How to develop a support group to which you can turn for support, honest, even harsh, feedback, and advice, and how to be able to do the same for others

k-o. One-on-one counseling and group counseling lab. In these five sessions, counselors practice offering both individual and group counseling based on problems and themes students face every day in our secondary school, as well as how to lead training groups for teachers, students, support staff, and parents. Here again, fellow counselors play the roles involved in each scenario. This is an important educative process in helping counselors walk the talk and understand what it is like to be on the receiving as well as the giving end of the helping process. Here are some examples of the kinds of one-on-one and group counseling themes that counselors will encounter in an effective intervention system. These practice sessions can be held after school and/or on weekends.

   • Overview of how to invite and counsel individual students; plan and lead intervention groups; sell and advertise groups to students, staff, and parents; and overcome resistance from reluctant counselees

   • Group for grieving peers of a popular ninth grade student who suddenly drowns

   • Group for students who were caught drunk at the homecoming dance and are required to attend group counseling for five sessions

- Group for eleventh grade students on how to become peer counselors
- Individual counseling with a male eleventh grade student being physically and emotionally abused by his mother's live-in boyfriend
- Group for ten students who are returning to school after thirty days of rehab for drug and alcohol addiction and have to undergo a five-session group counseling program
- A training group for teachers on how to become effective personal adult advocates
- A group for students who want to learn how to avoid partying on weekends and stay sober
- A group for stressed-out high achievers who are growing tired of the ongoing pressure from parents, teachers, and peers
- Individual counseling with a lesbian student who is being bullied by peers
- A group of students who are participating in a group to help stop or reduce their tobacco addiction
- Individual counseling with a female star athlete who has lost sixty pounds and resists intervention for anorexia
- A group for parents who want to learn more effective parenting skills and pass these skills along to other parents
- A group of marginal students seeking to turn their reputation as slackers in a more positive direction
- A group for support staff on how to become effective helpers
- Individual counseling with a male parent considering a divorce and worried about the impact on his two teen children

This example of a training curriculum based on data gathered from the counselor self-awareness inventory (see figure 3.1) provides counselors with a vehicle to begin sharing fundamental issues they are grappling with in the workplace, allowing them to come out from under their professional persona and become learners again. The principal, as head helper in the school, may also want to join in completing the inventory as a way to assess his own helping skills and levels of support. Principals are often the most isolated members of

The purpose of this inventory is to help you assess your strengths as a helper. The following questions will help you focus on the kinds of problems and people that elicit your best helping efforts. It will also help you identify the areas that are more difficult for you and need shoring up.

- What events or influences led you to want to help others?
- Who are your models and mentors? What did they teach you about the helping process? In particular, what words and actions did they use that made them stand out as effective helpers?
- Have you modeled your professional life after some of these valued mentors? Do you use some of the same skills or words you learned from these mentors in your own helping role? Can you still hear their voices?
- Often in our own development as persons and professionals we encounter helpers who are ineffective. While well meaning, they lack the skills and sometimes even the interest to be effective helpers. They often use words and actions that send the signal, "You'd better look elsewhere." Can you still hear their voices? Do you work not to become like them yourself? Please describe how these would-be helpers may have impacted on your life. They missed an opportunity. Did it hurt?
- What are your personal goals in helping others? In other words, what is in it for you? What do you think you will gain from the process?
- What are your fears about the helping process? We all come into the helping process a little uneasy. Questions abound. Will there be problems you feel you can't handle? Will your uneasiness with some clients come through?
- What kinds of people and groups do you prefer to help? In spite of the wise advice in our training that we need to be inclusive, we are still human and often our response is to maintain our own level of comfort. We tend to gravitate toward certain people and groups of people who don't threaten our professional and personal persona. Given this reality, we need to be aware of this tendency, see it clearly, so we don't avoid the "other" who may unsettle us. We need to constantly reassess our level of inclusion and work to expand, not limit, those we embrace. Do you like to help women, men, the elderly, younger people, the well educated, the economically well-off, the needy, the underdog, those left out of the mainstream, victims, and the like? Whom do you gravitate toward?
- What kinds of people and groups do you prefer not to help? We all have a dark side. We have a life experience in which we have been told to stay clear of some people and groups. The influence of our parents, peers, community, and culture may have placed limits on those whom we include and value. We are not always inclusive. For example, have you erected barriers with some clients because of age, gender, culture, color, personality, ethnicity, appearance, and the like? Whom do you avoid? Does it show?
- What kinds of problems interest you and motivate you to want to help? Again, our own background and experience often influence us to want to help with certain problems. Some examples might be problems with relationships, divorce, a gambling addiction, finances, abuse, loss and loneliness, anger and violence, and so on. What is your "preferred problem" list?
- What kinds of problems do you tend to avoid, refer to others, or bluntly say, "I don't do these kinds of problems"? For example, do you avoid suicide, health

Figure 3.1. Counselor Self-Awareness Inventory

issues such as anorexia and bulimia, extramarital affairs, grieving, and so on? What is your "I don't want to deal with this" list?

- Please list your strengths as a helper. For example, are you an effective listener and questioner, nonjudgmental, knowable, able to confront when needed, know when to end a counselor–client relationship and move on, able to establish a trusting and accepting relationship, refer and seek advice of a colleague or mentor when needed?
- We all have areas in which we lack skills or have skills that need improvement. We can never become the consummate professional without addressing these areas. Using a baseball analogy, we are like a pitcher who, while he has a good fastball, lacks a curve and a change-up. What skills do you lack? For example, do you need to learn to be less judgmental and a better listener, learn to engage problems you now avoid or refer, learn to confront when necessary, learn to end counseling relationships rather than hang onto them to satisfy your own personal needs, and so on?
- How do you view yourself as a professional helper? Are you good at this work or just getting along?
- How do others view you as a professional helper? For example, do colleagues see you as effective? How about your clients or students? And how about family members? Do they value your helping skills?
- Effective helpers often have an informal support group in which they can talk, receive feedback, and sound off about their professional and personal issues. It should come as no surprise that our professional and personal issues sometimes get meshed together. After all, when we help others we often become aware of our own personal issues that need attention. They persist and cry out for action. We are not immune to problems and suffer the same setbacks and problems that our clients face. Life hits us all. We are not much use to our clients and students if we are not working at resolving our own personal issues. To keep ourselves on an even keel, we need trusted colleagues and friends who can give us honest, sometimes even harsh, unpleasant, feedback. Please list at least ten people who currently serve, or could serve, as a support group for you. These are people who make time for you and are concerned about your personal and professional development, people who know your dark side and can quickly zero in when you are heading for conflict.

Figure 3.1. (*continued*)

the school community when it comes to asking for help and getting honest feedback.

8. Examining a state-of-the-art guidance and counseling program, using the RGSI to help raise the counseling staff's awareness of what services need addressing, and using the counselor self-awareness inventory (see figure 3.1) to aid the counseling staff in assessing their strengths and areas that need improvement can go a long way in helping counselors become aware of certain issues. For example, which students, parents, staff members, and issues or problems get

included and which get sidestepped or given a token response? In my experience once counselors have this information and awareness in hand, they are better positioned to begin taking the necessary steps to create clear open doors that students can walk through to get the help they need. If it is guidance for scheduling, test information, higher education, and career advising, those doors can be clearly marked. If it is for individual and group counseling support and information, those doors are also marked. And the doors through which teachers, students, support staff, and parents walk to get the training they need to help colleagues, peers, and fellow parents are also clearly marked. A familiar, welcoming counselor who is doing what he or she does as a helper mans each open door. There is no more mystery about what is in store, as compared to when students are assigned counselor by alphabet and grade.

Each high school is different and no one size fits the process of transforming guidance and counseling services. But I believe this process can work in many of our urban, suburban, and large centralized rural schools. Let's use Sachem North High School as an example. Currently there are eleven counselors assigned by alphabet in this grade 11–12 school. Instead of assigning counselors to students by alphabet, I argue it makes more sense to employ a differentiated staffing pattern based on the needs of students and counselor skills available to respond to those needs. This new configuration might include the following: six counselors to service scheduling, testing, college placement, and career guidance needs; three counselors to service the personal needs of students by offering individual and group counseling intervention; one counselor to service special education needs; one counselor to service the training needs of teachers, students, support staff, and parents.

In this scheme the principal is prepared to provide retraining to meet newly emerging needs of students, parents, and staff. The principal should also be prepared to help counselors mend some fences and open doors for potential helpers. They might be needed to close the schism between counselors who emerged as quasi-administrators charged with the selection and sorting of students into classes, higher education, and careers, and those counselors who, while well trained in the personal counseling role, literally found themselves having to put those skills on the shelf as they were not needed in the quasi-administrator role.

As a result, when students have personal issues such as eating disorders or facing the sudden death of a student, teacher, or parent; alcohol, drug, or alcohol addiction; physical, emotional, or sexual abuse; parental divorce; pressure from the college admission process; or students heading toward the margin or dropping out and so forth, these problems were often referred to community agencies, put on hold, or in the worst-case scenario, ignored. In my experience counselors forced into a bureaucratic role did not take kindly to their de facto removal from helping students with these personal issues. The role confusion cited by the ASCA between counselors trained in an education paradigm and those trained in a personal counseling paradigm was the product of a system that was based on the "my way or no way" thrust of the quasi-administrator role. The new differentiated staffing pattern I am arguing for allows both groups to come together as equal and valued partners, team members who each have a role to play.

The principal needs to lead an effort to help counselors mend fences between the guidance staff and teachers, students, support staff, parents, school nurses, social workers, and school psychologists. That means to begin to include the helping skills of all members of the school community as equal partners. For example, they must take an active role in training teachers to be personal adult advocates, to move away from the notion that only counselors know how to help students and teachers should stick to their academic role and stay out of the helping process.

The same can be said of students, support staff, and parents who want to be sources of help and referral to students headed for trouble. Counselors need to send a message to these groups that their involvement is valued and a necessary part of the schoolwide intervention system. Counselors will aid them in this process by offering training in the helping process. Finally, counselors will need to mend fences with school nurses, social workers, and school psychologists, not view them as competing professionals but rather members of the school helping team who bring unique resources to the schoolwide helping process, such as training teachers, students, support staff, and parent as helpers.

In the end the principal's message and expectation should be, "We are all in this together," a message that carries the expectation that every member of the school community is a potential source of help, advice, and referral. As reported in the Association for Supervision and Curriculum Development (ASCD) *Curriculum Update*, it is a message built on the counseling model of thirteen-year veteran Mark Kuranz, a counselor at J. I. Case High School in Racine, Wisconsin, who suggests, "A lot of times all kids want is someone to listen. It's a safe way for them to sort things out, to hear themselves. To me the key to being a good counselor is building relationships, with kids and families and staff and community members. Because once you have a relationship kids feel comfortable asking for help."[18]

Skilled counselors like Mark Kuranz understand they can't maintain an effective intervention system without building relationships with other members of the school community. Given the growing numbers of students experiencing personal and well-being problems that negatively impact on their academic performance, Kuranz and forward-thinking counselors understand they have to enlist the helping resources of every member of the school community—teachers, school nurses, support staff, parents, and administrators—in order to intervene to help every student and parent headed toward the margins of school life. They also understand that no new counseling resources are coming their way in this day of budget constraints.

As reported by education writer Shelly Reese, Patricia Martin, senior program manager for the Transforming School Counseling Initiative of Education Trust, suggests counselors must find effective ways to intercede on behalf of hundreds of students simultaneously. That requires different training and different strategies, she said. Vera Blake, principal of Holmes Middle School in Alexandria, Virginia, puts the problem in perspective by promoting and selling a philosophy that stresses identifying and involving all those who have a stake in the school's success.[19] As reported in the ASCD *Curriculum Update*, Blake suggests, "Our stakeholders are our students first, and we always try to keep them first, our faculty, parents, and community members." One clear-cut way for teachers, the school nurse, students, support staff, and parents to become dedicated stakeholders is for the principal to involve each group as helpers for marginal students.

Karen Gotwald, a seventh grade teacher at Roxboro Middle School in Cleveland Heights, Ohio, is an example of the emerging role of teachers as helpers and advocates. According to Shelly Reese, Gotwald uses picture books to spark discussion about death, divorce, and coping with disabilities. Gotwald, who has no formal training in counseling, said school is "no place to get territorial." When children's emotional development is at stake, "Kids need to go to the people they feel comfortable with. If a kid comes to me and says, 'My grandmother just died,' I can't just say, 'Well, sweetheart, I'm sorry, go sit down and open your book and do problems 1 through 16.' People say they don't know how to find time but if I don't fit in a few minutes for that child, they're not going to hear a word I say."

Patricia Martin's argument that counselors need to employ different training and strategies points to the need for teachers like Gotwald to play a major role in the helping. Martin gives an excellent example of the need for alternatives when counseling resources are limited. She states that in many schools with fewer than six hundred students, there is only one counselor. To say that counselor is going to be available to handle the mental health needs of six hundred students is almost insanity.

The remaining sections of the chapter focus on how the principal involves caring and concerned teachers like Karen Gotwald, as well as school nurses, students, support staff, and parents to aid in the counseling process.

TRAINING TEACHERS TO BECOME PERSONAL ADULT ADVOCATES

I believe the *Breaking Ranks 11* recommendation that each student have a personal adult advocate to help him or her personalize the educational experience is right on target. Every school, every child, and every parent could benefit from having a faculty member who meets with a student on

a regular basis; who knows his or her aspirations, strengths, and weaknesses; and who communicates with the student's teachers and parents,
even those parents who are hard to reach and resistant to intervention by
the school. This kind of personalized schooling and oversight is just what
is needed in our large high schools that invite anonymity and isolation
on the part of every member of the school community—administrators,
teachers, students, and parents.

Richard Scardamaglia, superintendent in the Rincon Valley Union
School District in Santa Rosa, California, provides us with the kind of
benefits that can emerge for both teachers and students when teachers are
utilized as personal adult advocates.[20] Scardamaglia reports:

> The Student Advocate program releases teachers from classroom duties for
> three to four hours per week to work with students on a one-on-one basis.
> The students are sometimes labeled "at risk" but they can be any child who
> needs extra attention or a trusted friend to talk to. The advocate's role is sim-
> ply to be a good listener, a big brother or sister. Often this is enough to help
> a child through a rough period in his or her life.
>
> With a ratio of one counselor per 700 students, our counselors cannot
> possibly meet all the demands of our student population. While most teach-
> ers already supply some of the extra emotional support that our students
> need in their classrooms, some problems demand more time than a teacher
> can give in the few minutes before school, between classes or during recess.
> Teacher advocates are not intended to take the place of counselors or thera-
> pists although they do receive training in crisis intervention. When serious
> issues arise, we have clear guidelines for referring the child to the appro-
> priate support person or agency. Perhaps the greatest praise for the program
> has come from administrators and teachers in other districts who have asked
> us to help them develop their own advocate program. The Student Advocate
> program is one of those rare ideas that are both simple and inexpensive to
> implement. The beauty of the program is that it capitalizes on the closeness
> and trust that already exist between students and teachers.

However, Scardamaglia's positive assessment of the student advocate
program omits some of the complex issues he and his staff faced when implementing the program. For example, how did they get reluctant and resistant teachers to get on board and add an advising component to their
daily work? How did they proceed to sell parents on the need for this kind
of enhanced teacher–student relationship? How were counselors, social

workers, and school psychologists persuaded to share their intervention work with teachers? And how were teacher advocates trained, supported, and mentored as they encountered their own problems in helping students on a personal level? This is the kind of grounded information principals need if they are going to prepare teachers for the professional and political realities involved when teachers take on a personal helping role, to avoid the trap of merely sending them on their way and hoping for the best.

Researcher Pedro A. Noguera reminds us that simply telling teachers that they are now student advisors or personal adult advocates without training and commitment is a plan doomed to failure for students, teachers, parents, and administrators involved. As principals envision a plan of how to harness the helping skills of teachers, I urge them to keep in mind Noguera's observation that, "The schools' attempts to personalize school through an advisory system, in which teachers served as student counselors through an extended homeroom period held once each week, seemed equally ineffective. We sat in on several advisory classes where no advising was occurring. The teachers had no idea of how to use the allotted time, and most lacked experience in counseling." As Noguera suggests, it comes as no surprise that 80 percent of the students said "no" when asked, "Is there an adult in your school to whom you would turn if you were experiencing a serious personal problem?" And 56 percent of the students said they did not believe anyone cared about how well they did in school.[21]

But Noguera's observations of a failing teacher-led advising system offers some useful insights into where principals need to begin the process of getting teachers on board as personal student advocates when he states that the teachers obviously had no idea how to use the allotted time, most lacked experience in counseling, and no advising was occurring. Preparing teachers to be effective personal adult advocates begins by providing them with counseling and advising skills; showing them how to model the helping process; teaching them how to facilitate individual and group meetings with students or parents; and teaching them how to make the maximum use of the allotted time so these individual and group sessions become ongoing learning opportunities for both students and teachers.

Principals also need to keep in mind that the shift from academic teacher to personal student advocate will be a big leap for many teachers and will involve setbacks and failures. Simply put, teachers tend to rely on a lecture format and emphasis on delivery of content, while the person in the role of personal student advocate relies on listening, accepting, clarifying, suggesting alternatives, modeling, advocating with other teachers, administrators, and parents, setting up referrals when needed, providing support, developing a close personal relationship with each student, and being perceived as an adult with real-life experiences who can be counted on to be available when trouble looms.

There is a great deal to learn and many skills to master for the potential student adult advocate. By first reorganizing the guidance and counseling services and freeing up counselors with training and individual/group counseling skills, the principal has created a ready-made resource to lead a personal adult advocate training program that can give teachers counseling techniques and skills such as listening, clarifying, confronting, supporting, and so on. This is a training experience that can have a major impact not only on the ways teachers advise students but also on their teaching performance, the ways in which they relate to colleagues in the school community, and their stake, ownership, and value in their school's success. Personal student advocates can use these newly acquired skills in their daily classroom teaching to be more inclusive and reach out to reluctant and resisting learners. The school principal, by modeling and advocating staff members to utilize these skills, can help create a school community where there is a high level of open communication, respect, caring, and support among colleagues regardless of their differences.

The acquiring of these counseling-like skills, therefore, can serve as a vehicle to help implement the recommendations of the *Breaking Ranks 11* report, such as teachers conveying a sense of caring to their students so that students feel that their teachers share a stake in their learning; teachers being adept at acting as coaches and facilitators to promote active involvement of students in their own learning; and a high school regarding itself as a community in which members of the staff collaborate to develop and implement the school's learning goals. Caring, facilitating, and collaborating can only emerge when staff members are given training in how to be effective listeners, caring, accepting of the differences of others, being able to suggest alternative solutions to problems, and being advocates and developing close and intimate collaborative relations not only with students but also with colleagues and other members of the school community.

In my experience in training teachers as personal student advocates, another important by-product is that teachers begin to feel they have a major role to play in advising students and are not being displaced by a layer of multiple services led by specialists such as counselors, school psychologists, and social workers. They once again have a stake and responsibility in what happens to their students and can reap the personal and professional rewards that come with helping as well as teaching students and, as important, collaborating with colleagues such as counselors who are now seen as peers rather than quasi-administrators. It often follows that in the process, teachers who have doubted their helping abilities and responsibility begin to regain their confidence that they indeed can be personal adult advocates who have legitimate helping skills and don't have to quickly refer every troubled student.

Training teachers as personal student advocates has a benefit in that it has something useful to offer students, teachers, and the entire school community. It is an opportunity to open new doors between teachers and students, teachers and colleagues, and an opportunity to expand the ways in which members of the school community communicate, collaborate, and care for each other. Education critic and author Seymour Sarason reminds us that whatever factor, variables, and ambience are conducive for the growth, development, and self-regard of students are precisely those that are crucial to obtaining the same consequences for a school staff. Education writer Bonnie Bernard also offers some wise advice when she says, "It's hard to be caring and supportive, to have high expectations, and to involve students in decision making without support, respect, opportunities to work collegially with others. Fostering resiliency in young people is ultimately an inside-out process that depends on educators taking care of themselves. To see strengths in children, we must see our strengths; to look beyond their risks and see their resiliency means acknowledging our own inner resiliency."[22] Training teachers to be personal adult advocates creates the conditions where teachers can begin to see their strengths and their own inner resiliency; it is a way to move teachers out of the box of being an observer or nonparticipant in the helping process and into a leadership role. It is also a way, as Patricia Martin suggests, for school counselors to find effective ways to intercede on behalf of hundreds of students simultaneously by harnessing the helping resources of teachers, recognizing that different training and strategies are required to respond to the growing personal and well-being problems of students and parents.[23]

Here is an example of a six-step training program to train teachers as personal student advocates that principals can implement, utilizing the training skills of a team of in-house counselors, school nurse, social worker, school psychologist, and the principal himself or herself. This is a beginning step in the process and the principal will also need to set up an ongoing support network for teachers as they encounter setbacks and resistance as well as successes. One approach is to assign each of the trainers to be mentors as the program evolves, a mentoring situation in which teachers, as do their students, meet regularly on a one-on-one or group basis to discuss the issues they are encountering, share their newly learned helping skills, and learn new skills that are needed in the ever-changing school environment. Here is the training program:

1. Training teachers to help. In this beginning session, the counselor/ trainer demonstrates to teachers how to make initial contact with students, set boundaries for the helping relationship, hold a helping conversation, and end the helping relationship when the student seems better. Teachers learn that the helping relationship begins by talking to the student in simple ways: "Hi, John, how are things with your parents' divorce? Let's get a burger together and talk about how you are doing," and explaining to the student that while the teacher/ helper will do what he or she can to help the situation, he or she may have to refer the student to the counselor if the problems worsen. Teachers also learn how to end a helping relationship when the student seems better able to handle the situation or is referred for more help. Simple words work best: "John, it looks like things are better for you now that the divorce is over and you and your mom have a new start. I'll be close by if things take a turn for the worse."

2. Training teachers to listen. Listening is the teacher/helper's most important skill in the intervention process. Teachers need to learn that they must be ready and able to hear a student's concerns. The old adage applies: "Don't ask how someone feels if you don't want them to tell you." And teachers need to be ready to accept what the student has to say regardless of the content. If a student shares a fear about her father's physical abuse of her mother, the teacher/helper

can't say, "I don't do abuse problems." The role of the teacher/ helper is to hear the full story, assess what can be done, and, if a referral is necessary, say to the student, "I think we need more help with this problem. Let me call in Dr. Jones from the guidance department. I think he can help us to solve this problem much faster."

3. Training teachers to be aware of problems that could face students. Many adolescents experience problems related to family crisis, peer rejection, school failure, truancy, death and loss, suicide issues, physical and sexual abuse, eating disorders, and alcohol, drug, and tobacco abuse. Teachers learn about the dynamics in each of these problem clusters and how to anticipate how they would respond to students troubled by these issues. A useful technique is for teachers to share how they resolve some of these problems in their own lives. How were they helped? What worked? Teachers are also reminded that these problems can affect any student, regardless of ability and income. In fact, the most gifted and talented students may be the most in need because it is hard for them, customarily, to ask for help because so much is expected of them. Teachers are also reminded that these problems are life's problems and they must work hard not to be frightened by them. Their role is to get the troubled student help, either by their own efforts or in conjunction with other resources. If students are frightened by their own situations, it doesn't do them any good to talk to a helper who is also frightened.

4. Confronting fears about the helping process. The trainers should stress that advising young people can be complicated. There are risks in becoming too involved with students. Effective helpers establish professional boundaries. They are not therapists, parents, or friends of students. They should avoid spending too much time with individual students and meeting them outside of school. When helpers act as messiahs, they can further complicate a student's life, present false hopes of caring, and risk misconduct.

5. Training teachers to make good referrals. Teacher/helpers need to know when to refer and how to go about the referral process. In this session teachers are encouraged to trust their own judgment when they feel they cannot help the student. They need to be reminded that there are times when students do need professional help. Teachers learn to be straightforward and clear when a referral is in

order. Simple words work best: "Sandy, you are in physical danger
with your mom's boyfriend drinking and acting as he does. We need
to act together, right now, to get you and your mom help. I am calling social services and asking them for an immediate response."
Simple statement, but delivered with clout. No "maybes" or "let's
wait until tomorrow." The teacher/helper acts now.

6. The teacher/helper learns to be part of the school's helping team. In
   this final session, teachers are encouraged to think of themselves as
   a primary resource in the school's helping process. Teachers are reminded that each teacher/helper, along with the counselors and administrators, brings a unique helping skill to the team. Some team
   members are gifted helpers. Others are less gifted but continue to
   learn. Teachers are reminded that it is okay for them to seek out the
   help and advice of fellow teachers, counselors, and administrators as
   they immerse themselves in the helping process.

It is hoped that administrators, counselors, and teacher leaders at the
school level will add their own unique approaches to the steps I have presented. How this plan works in individual schools will depend on the will,
commitment, vision for change, and leadership skills of the school administrators. It will also depend on counselors accepting and understanding that in turning over some of their resources to teachers they are max-
imizing their leverage as helpers. Finally, it will depend on leadership
from teacher leaders who realize that teachers need to play a more powerful role in helping troubled students.

TRAINING STUDENTS, SUPPORT STAFF, AND
PARENTS TO BE HELPERS

Having transformed the guidance and counseling services and brought
teachers on board as personal student advocates, the principal's next step
in creating a schoolwide intervention system is to enlist students, support
staff, and parents as sources of help and referral on the front lines of the
school and community. Students, support staff, and parents are really the
eyes and ears of what is going on in the school and community. They are
often the first to observe students like Taylor Hooton and J. Daniel

Scruggs, who are on the fast track to troubled lives. They can also sense the huge loss felt by the entire school community when sudden death comes to students like Rob Pace and Calvin Kohart. And they are often the first to observe parents like Judith Scruggs, who needed early intervention and support before her son hanged himself. Yet, incredibly, the helping resources of students, support staff, and parents are not called upon in our large secondary schools.

Consider for a moment the helping and referring potential of a high school having 2,000 students, perhaps 200 support staff, and a parent population of more than 3,000. Imagine the huge opportunities each student, support staff person, and parent has each day to offer support, advice, and sources of referral, if—and this is the rub in most schools—they are asked to be aware of students headed for trouble, trained in simple helping techniques, expected to be critical members of the school's intervention team, and have an open door the students can walk through to share a concern or their need for advice on how to help others from a trusted personal adult advocate, counselor, school nurse, social worker, school psychologist, or community counselor.

This kind of invitation and inclusion in the school's intervention team also serves as a valuable learning experience for students, support staff, and parents. That is, in helping other people they can accrue many personal benefits, such as learning more about themselves in terms of the kinds of people and problems they tend to engage or push away, come to the realization that their own problems and issues are more similar than different, and that being responsive to others tends to raise their own self-esteem, personal risk-taking, and self-worth.

Anyone who has experienced observing a person helping a troubled student or parent knows this role can build pride and make the helping person feel useful and an important member of the school community. This is particularly true for students who find that they are learning the personal helping skills that are so needed by adults in our increasingly anonymous world. The process also serves to provide an ongoing pool of informal helpers who are aware of the ever-changing needs of students and parents in the school community, serving as a critical backup team to the school's professional helpers. In a sense enlisting the helping resources of students, support staff, and parents is a deliberate move by the principal to meet the recommendation of the *Breaking Ranks 11* report that a high school will regard itself as a community whose goal is to increase the quantity and improve the quality of interactions between students and, I would suggest, to increase the quantity and improve the quality of interactions between students, support staff, and parents as well.

The vehicle for increasing the quantity and improving the quality of interactions is actively engaging students, support staff, and parents in the process. However, the principal, in formulating his or her vision of how best to include each member of the school community in the intervention process, needs to keep in mind that he or she is not simply advocating helping others as a feel-good activity. His or her message should be more about active participation and using the helping process to provide yet another open door for troubled students and parents, a process that serves to encourage students, support staff, and parents to move away from their own self-interest and focus on personal gains and begin participating in the problem-solving activities of other school community members. He or she must encourage them to learn to understand the struggles and rewards that come with deciding to be of use and service to others, using their talents to affect the slide of students and parents toward the margins, and participating in their lives in a meaningful and helpful way.

They must learn to use the helping process as a model for participation and engagement in other aspects of community life that require intervention to, again, increase the quantity and improve the quality of interactions among the varying political and cultural groups in the community. The principal needs to communicate that this process is particularly helpful for the marginal students and parents who, by participating in the process of helping others, find a path to becoming a responsive and responsible member of the school community. They learn to use the helping process as an open door through which they can walk to find their own voice and value, meaningful activity in helping others, and a sense of belonging and positive connection with other community members, and cultivate a sense that they are involved in an activity that is important and of value.

Finally, the principal needs to envision a multilevel approach to enlisting the helping resources of students, support staff, and parents. His or her first step should be to use his or her position to encourage students to pay attention to their peers and when they see a student headed for the margins, seek out a trusted professional staff member to share their concerns. Second, the principal needs to provide short-term training in the helping process for students who can serve as peer counselors, support staff, and parents who can serve as sources of outreach to help other parents. The same training model can be used separately for students, support staff, and parents. Here is an example of a two-part simplified training program.

Part one involves consideration of three case studies involving students David, Mike, Valerie, and Samantha; their parents Rita, Mike, Maureen, and Amy; their grandparents Kevin, Arlene, and Al, and Uncle Dennis. These case studies provide future helpers with the opportunity to reflect on how they might intervene to help students and parents going through similar troubles, such as the death of a loved one, addiction of a parent, or serious illness of a grandparent.

Part two involves future helpers completing my student–support staff–parent helper inventory, which I adapted from my counselor self-awareness inventory and personal adult advocate training process. The material elicited from conversations about the case studies and data from the inventory sets the stage for an in-depth discussion of how to approach troubled students and parents. This training program can be used in helping programs that already exist in many schools, such as athletes helping athletes, leadership training, training for diversity, and peer counseling.

The training can also be used to enhance parent training programs such as the Phoenix Country Day School in Phoenix, Arizona. As reported by Shelly Reese, John Crabb, division head for the middle grades, reports that although there are ample resources for counseling, Phoenix Country Day augments its traditional counseling program with training for parents. Several times a year, Crabb sponsors informal meetings where he describes the social dynamics of middle school life and gives parents tips about reducing peer pressure and promoting inclusiveness. Mr. Crabb might want to consider the training suggested here as an additional tool in promoting inclusiveness and reducing peer pressure, not only for students but also for parents and support staff, some of whom are living on the margins of school life.

Here are the case studies; the inventory appears in figure 3.2.

Case # 1

David is a sixteen-year-old high school student. His father, Peter, after battling lung cancer for over two years, passed away in a hospice last

Section I: Introduction to the Helping Process
1. Give an example of how you have been helped with a problem by another person.
2. What helping skills did this person use well? For example, were they non-judgmental and did not give advice?
3. Give an example of how you were not helped with a problem by another person.
4. What helping skills did this person lack? For example, the person told you how they solved a similar problem and didn't appear to listen to your concerns.
5. How do you rate your own helping skills? Are they good, adequate, mediocre, sometimes a failure?
6. What helping skills do you lack? For example, being able to listen to and help peers whom you find different and difficult to relate to.
7. What kinds of students do you like to help? For example, do you work best with students who are well behaved, attentive, and interested in solving their problems?
8. What kinds of students do you have trouble helping and tend to avoid? For example, do you find yourself avoiding students who don't seem to listen or care about the group or solving their problems?
9. What has been the most rewarding part of the helping experience for you?
10. What has been a nightmare or, at the very least, bothersome about the helping experience?
11. What teachers, peers, or other adults have been sources of support for you?
12. What do your parent(s) or guardian(s) say about your desire to help others? What do you tell them?
13. Often when we help others we become more aware of our own self and our problems. Helping others raises our self-awareness. Name one problem you have and how you are going about solving the problem . . . or avoiding the problem.

Section II: The Skills We Need to be Effective Helpers
1. How do you make contact with students (or parents) who need help?
2. How do you get them to talk about a concern?
3. How do you observe nonverbal communication? For example, body language that suggests that they are uncomfortable and would prefer not to speak.
4. How do you listen and show genuine empathy?
5. How do you remain nonjudgmental?
6. How do you refrain from giving advice?
7. How do you get troubled students (and parents) to see that everyone gets hurt by life and has problems, not just them?
8. How do you maintain and value privacy?
9. How do you handle the following kinds of problems that may emerge in helping others? Give short responses to each problem area.
   - Family concerns:
   - Alcohol and drug problems:
   - School problems (such as school failure):
   - Peer problems:
   - Sexual problems:
   - Abuse problems:
   - Eating disorders:

Figure 3.2. Student–Support Staff–Parent Helper Inventory

- Loss (such as death or divorce):
- Suicidal concerns:
10. When and how do you refer someone for more help?
11. When you have a concern as a helper, how do you get support?

Section III: Training Group Role-Playing
Group Role-Play #1: Have each member give an example of how he or she was helped with a personal problem by another person.
Group Role-Play #2: Have each member give an example of how he or she was not helped by another person.
Group Role-Play #3: Have each member give an example of how his or her privacy was violated by another person.
Group Role-Play #4: Have members give an example of what they did when they found out they couldn't handle a problem by themselves.
Group Role-Play #5: Have each member give an example of how he or she was judged by another person.
Group Role-Play #6: Have each member give an example of a problem he or she is experiencing as a helper.

Figure 3.2. *(continued)*

week. David is a shy, withdrawn student with few friends. He is an only child. He has spent most of his after-school time playing computer games with his dad and helping his mom, Rita, with preparing dinner, medications, and so on. Rita, an RN, works the night shift at Southside Hospital. David has been her rock. An observer might say he is another adult in the home, not a teenager, taking over while Rita works to help make ends meet. But last week, all of David and Rita's outpouring of love, help, caring, and anger came to an end. And all the pain, regrets, "why me?" questions, and struggles with saying good-bye came to an end for Peter. Peace, if you can call it that, comes to each of them. The hospice people know how to help people through these last moments. Yes, everything was in place. The final arrangements were made. Peter's suit was ready for the wake. Friends rushed to offer support, care, and sustenance. What to do with all the leftover food and flowers? The business of dying takes over and the grief and anger get put on hold.

However, Rita, being a caring mom, knows she and David are going to need help to work through the loss of Peter and learn to adjust to their new life, a life without the daily stress of illness, dreams put on hold, refilling what seemed to be a million medications to help Peter fight off the pain, and relatives, friends, and neighbors asking, "How is he doing? He'll be all right. He's tough. We're praying for him." Rita knows that learning how to live again, maybe even love again, will not come easy for her. It's been a long time since she was held and felt feminine, wanted, and wanting. And she knows that David will now be left with a great void and sense of loss. He lost his only friend, his dad.

Rita fears that she and David might end up just clinging to each other, with the memory of Peter always there. Rita doesn't want to see that happen. She acts. She calls the school counselor and asks her to talk to David and to let his teachers know that it is going to be a hard time for him. He is going to need friends and new activities, live life without a burden for a change. He needs to date, go to dances, invite friends to his house, and so on. Rita wants so much for David. But she also knows it will not be easy for him. He's going to need a lot of help.

Rita also calls a counselor she knows from the hospital who specializes in grieving and loss. She needs someone who can help her with all the new decisions coming her way, like how to: gather up Peter's clothing and belongings; deal with money issues; consider moving to a smaller home or maybe a condo; deal with Peter's parents and siblings, who are already trying to run her life; think about joining a group for widows and widowers; maybe even take a vacation with David to get away from it all for a while. And yes, how to be a person in her own right, who is no longer burdened and frightened, to wake up in the morning and see sunlight and flowers and have some hope. She must learn to love Peter's memory but let him go.

Case # 2

Michael, or Mike as he is known in the family and on the force, is a forty-four-year-old patrolman. He has been married to Maureen for twenty-four years. They have a son, Michael Jr., age seventeen, and a daughter, Valerie, age fifteen. Mike comes from a police family. His dad, Kevin, now retired, is a decorated detective. Mike's older brother, Dennis, is a sergeant in homicide. Mike has been offered promotions but prefers to stay on patrol as he has a carpentry business on the side that is booming. The two brothers and father are very close. They have season tickets to the Jets, Knicks, Mets, and the Long Island Ducks. Kevin also has a Boston Whaler and the boys, as they are called, spend a lot of time on the Great South Bay fishing and, one of the family's favorite pastimes, drinking.

You might say Mike comes from a drinking family. Family parties for weddings, birthdays, baptisms, funerals, and graduations are lively events with lots of beer, wine, and liquor consumed. Over the past few years Maureen had become concerned abut Mike's drinking. He often had to be driven home by Kevin or a family friend after a night of drinking at a game or at a favorite police bar. Sometimes he becomes violent when Maureen expresses her fears about his drinking; fights would follow with yelling and Maureen being pushed or punched. As the kids grew older, they often intervened to pull Mike away. He promised over and over to sober up and stop hitting Maureen, but nothing changed. Everyone—the kids, Maureen—went his or her own ways and avoided Mike as he continued to drink more and more. He drank so much that he was increasingly too hung over to go to work. He became irresponsible as a husband, father, and worker.

The word got around. Everyone in the police department knew Mike had a drinking problem. It takes a lot for professionals to address, up front, the growing addiction of a coworker. We look the other way, thinking it's not our job to confront drunks and druggies, even when they are endangering their lives, the lives of those they are supposed to help, and even the lives of their own family. Then, time ran out on Mike. His supervisor, Captain Martinez, had seen enough. He called Mike to his office, along with a representative from the PBA, and said that Mike's continued absenteeism, poor work performance, and word of his drunkenness at police parties indicated that Mike needed help, right now. Captain Martinez suggested that it would be in the best interests of Mike, his family, the department, and the PBA for Mike to enter a thirty-day rehab at the Hazelden Clinic in Center City, Minnesota. Arrangements had been made for an early morning flight the next day to Minneapolis. A Hazelden counselor would meet Mike at the airport. His job was secure if he acted on this request. Mike met privately with the PBA rep, who strongly suggested that Mike buy into this offer.

That night Mike went home and told Maureen, Valerie, and Mike Jr. It was a sad and tearful night but they all slept more peacefully, feeling, at last, that God had sent them some help, a way out of this mess. Before going to bed Mike called his father and brother and told them the news. Both men disagreed and told Mike, "You're no drunk and they can't push a good cop around like this. Our family has a proud record. We'll help you fight this fuckin' shit." But Mike knew if he didn't get on that plane he would drink more and really hit bottom and lose his wife and kids and his job. There was no more hiding behind the bottle.

Mike also received a call from the counselor at Hazelden, who praised Mike for his decision and shared information about the Hazelden program. He also spoke with Maureen and indicated that he would be talking with her at least once a week. He said she would be flying out to meet with Mike and the Hazelden staff during the last few days of the rehab period. He also recommended that once Mike returned from rehab, she too become involved with the Hazelden outreach Mike would be attending in Bay Shore. He urged Maureen to call the school counseling office, tell them about Mike's rehab plan, and have them schedule Mike Jr. and Valerie for counseling. He asked that the school counselor call him at Hazelden so they could work together to prepare a plan of intervention for Mike Jr. and Valerie. A plan of help for each family member was evolving.

Case # 3

Arlene is in a tough spot. Now sixty-eight years old and recently retired from teaching, she looked forward to traveling with her husband and spending more time with her granddaughter Samantha. But things aren't working out that way. Her hopes and dreams have been literally destroyed over the past year and she feels she is being destroyed in the process. What happened to those dreams, you ask? Just after the Christmas holidays last year, she and Al were planning their first vacation trip to Puerto Rico. But almost overnight, Al suddenly began to lose his memory. It began with his forgetting his way home. Then there was a series of auto accidents in which he had no recollection of what happened.

The family doctor advised Arlene not to worry, that Al was in good health and this was, he hoped, a passing thing. But Al began to drink more and more, to follow Arlene around the house and question what she was doing, where she was going, and to whom she was talking on the telephone. It became a never-ending ordeal for Arlene. Her loving husband was turning into a nightmare for both Arlene and himself. Here was a successful, alert businessman, spending his days in a bathrobe, sleeping, talking to himself. What was happening? Arlene was terrified.

But Arlene was a doer and a provider. She didn't bother others with her troubles. Finally, at the end of her rope, she called her daughter Amy for advice. Amy, married to Tom and mother of eleven-year-old Samantha, lived in a nearby community. Amy had been so busy with New Year's parties and then back to her work as a first-grade teacher that she hadn't seen her mom and dad since their Christmas Day get together. So she was shocked by her mother's description of what was happening. After school she rushed over and found her dad completely depressed and unable to hold a conversation with her. Amy recognized that the situation was spinning out of control rapidly. She had heard of Alzheimer's disease and how it could come on suddenly, but why was this happening to her lovely dad? She urged her mom to call the family doctor and insist on a complete assessment at St. Catherine's Hospital in Smithtown, which had an Alzheimer's facility.

The assessment was not good. Al indeed had a rapidly progressing case of Alzheimer's. Dr. Myers, the consulting physician, indicated that Al would need a day-care program right away, a setting in which he could participate in daily activities that would hopefully help him to keep some degree of focus and also help Arlene have some relief. He cautioned Arlene that a caregiver like her could easily become worn down and ill herself. However, Dr. Myers warned that the day-care program was only a temporary fix. Al would need a permanent placement at St. Catherine's within the next year, at most. His advice to Arlene and Amy was, "Best to start making plans now, get the paperwork in, and help prepare yourself for this eventuality. It's going to happen sooner rather than later. Al needs this kind of twenty-four-hour care. You can't do it on your own."

Arlene and Amy left in tears. What was Amy going to tell Samantha about Grandpa? They had enjoyed such a warm and loving relationship. "I am so proud of my little girl," Al would always say. They would talk on the phone at least once a week and Al would attend Samantha's soccer games. Samantha had asked Amy why Grandpa wasn't calling, was anything wrong. Now she had to be told the truth. But Arlene said, "Please, not now, maybe the doctor is wrong. Maybe Dad will come around and be all right. These things do happen. I'll pray, make him eat more, take him out for rides. I know I can help him. Please just tell Samantha that Grandpa is not feeling well right now but he'll call soon. Please, Amy. I need to give Dad, and myself, one more chance. I have to do it."

And so it went, Arlene trying everything she knew to shake Al out of his deep depression. She tried the adult day-care in Hauppauge, but Al just

sat and cried all day. The counselor there said that this was not, as she described it, "an appropriate placement." So Al stayed at home, sat and
stared at Arlene, and followed her throughout the house. She became a
prisoner, escaping for only a few minutes to go out and buy food. She then
tried having a caretaker come in to help, a gentle and caring woman. But
Al yelled curses and threw things at her. After a week she said she could
not allow herself to be treated like that and she left. Yelling? Using curse
words? Al never yelled and never said so much as a damn. Arlene cried
herself to sleep knowing the man beside her was not "her Al" any more.

But she couldn't let him go. Amy and Tom kept pressuring her, saying
she could no longer care for Dad. One day Amy unexpectedly brought
Samantha over, saying, "She has to see Dad. It's not right to keep her in
the dark. She knows something is wrong. It's time, Mom, for her, for us,
to move on." And so Samantha sat with Al. For a few moments he seemed
to remember her. He hugged her and kissed her and said, "I've been sick.
I'm still sick. I'm sorry, my little girl." He sat holding her hand while
Samantha, Amy, and Arlene just cried. It seemed as if he were slowly dying in front of them. He had left them.

After Al fell asleep, Amy, Samantha, and Arlene sat around the kitchen
table and reminisced about the happier days with Dad/Grandpa/Al. Then
Arlene said, "I know I have to place him in the hospital but I don't know
if I can do it. I need help. It's so hard. It's killing me to see him as he is
but it's also killing me to have him leave me."

Amy replied by saying:

The hospital has a counselor ready to help you sort out your feelings. I
talked to her this morning. Ms. Kelly is her name. She sounds very nice. Her
job is to help families like us deal with these situations. Maybe I shouldn't
be doing this but I made an appointment with her for tomorrow morning at
10:00. I'll take the day off to watch over Dad. I am going to see Ms. Kelly
on Saturday to help work through my own feelings on this whole thing. And
Samantha and I have talked about her seeing the middle school counselor to
work through her feelings about Grandpa. I know she wants to visit him if
he does go into the hospital but I also know these places are difficult for
young kids to see. So Mom, this is something we have to do and do now for
Dad. He's done so much for us. We can't let him down when he is in such
turmoil. Let's try to restore some dignity for him and give both of you some

peace. You've done all you can. You need a respite so you can be ready for this next phase of both your lives. I am so sorry but we can't just cry. I'll see you at 8:00 tomorrow morning so you'll have time to dress. Look your best, baby! Deal? It's game time, Mom.

Arlene understood and thanked Amy for making the call to Ms. Kelly, a call she knew was needed but was unable to make. "Yes," she said quietly, "it's time."

USING THE COORDINATED SCHOOL HEALTH PROGRAM (CSHP) TO ENHANCE THE ROLE OF THE SCHOOL NURSE

The final step for the principal in bringing his or her intervention system into the twenty-first century is reorganizing the school's nursing program. This final step, as with the other components of a schoolwide intervention system, must begin with envisioning new open doors and strategies that can best address health and well-being problems of students and their families. That process must include analyzing the link between students headed toward the margins and the development of health-related problems. As Lisa Berkman, a researcher for the Robert Woods Johnson Foundation, suggests, people who are isolated tend to smoke more and be more overweight and less physically active.[24]

Social isolation, the feeling of disconnection, of not belonging, is a chronically stressful experience that has a direct biological effect on the body. We need more than one person in our world to make things work. Berkman argues that we need social networks in which people can surround themselves with others who encourage healthy choices, networks that can become a natural part of one's life. In a real sense, increasing the quantity and quality of students' access to health issues is the final building block, open door, in helping redirect marginal students to full membership in the school community. It rounds out the intervention blanket of care that provides open doors for help offered by personal counselors, teachers who are personal adult advocates, and student/support staff/ parent helpers, a process that enables the school community to quickly assess the personal, academic, health, and well-being problems of each student and quickly intervene when trouble appears. It is a process that combines quality education, support services, parent involvement, and access to community health and social service agencies.

As the Department of Health and Human Services 2003 report *Stories from the Field: Lessons Learned about Building Coordinated School Health Programs* suggests, by addressing health-related issues, schools not only foster students' academic achievement but also help establish healthy behaviors that can last a lifetime.[25] Young people spend more time in school than any other place but home, and schools have more influence on their lives than any other social institution but the family. Each school day in the United States, about 53 million young people attend 117,000 elementary and secondary schools for about six hours of classroom time. In the school setting, behaviors are developed and reinforced that will govern actions for a lifetime.

The lessons students learn in school about high-risk behaviors can affect not only their present health and their success in school but also their health and productivity as adults. The report also states that the Centers for Disease Control and Prevention (CDC) have identified key health-risk behaviors that are preventable, such as tobacco use; unhealthy eating; inadequate physical activity; alcohol and drug use; sexual behaviors that result in HIV infection, other sexually transmitted diseases, or unintended pregnancy; and behaviors that result in violence and unintentional injuries, including those sustained in motor vehicle accidents. Schools can play a key role in reducing the effects of these preventable behaviors, not only while young people are students but throughout their lives. The report highlights the three critical arguments I have raised in this book.

One, there is a relationship between students headed toward the margins of school life and the potential to develop health-related problems, citing research that confirms relationships between many health-risk behaviors and negative outcomes such as absenteeism, dropout rates, and poor school performance. Argument two focuses on the degree to which students feel positively connected to school being strongly related to whether they achieve academically or engage in activity that might put them at risk.

The report indicates that researchers have identified protective factors or developmental assets that can reduce health-risk factors. These include students' sense of "connectedness" to their families, schools, and communities; their involvement in the community; their access to community resources; and the amount of time spent with their families. Argument three is my suggestion that although the primary mission of any school is education, schools can no longer ignore the personal, health, and well-being factors that adversely affect students.

The *Stories from the Field* report calls for a "coordinated school health program" to address these concerns. The coordinated school health program consists of components that interact to function as a unified system, such as the intervention system I describe in this book. And as I suggest in this book, each intervention component contains key staff members who are responsible and responsive, such as individual and group counselors, counselors who serve as trainers, teacher leaders who oversee the personal adult advocates, school nurse, social workers, school psychologists, and building administrator. The coordinated school health program suggested by the CDC includes the following:

- Comprehensive school health education
- Physical education
- School health services
- School nutrition services
- School counseling, psychological, and social services
- Family and community involvement in the schools

Stories from the Field concludes that the good news is that many of the components of a coordinated school health program are already incorporated in some schools. However, what most schools do not have is a system in which the components work together to ensure that all students practice health-promoting behaviors.

The recommendations by the CDC for a coordinated school health program (CSHP) provides needed support to my argument that time is passing by the school nurse model that serves only to react and respond to the daily needs of students. That model is slowly being replaced by a system that has a major focus on early assessment, diagnosis, speedy intervention, and prevention. Prevention connects the school nurse to other CSHP team members such as health and physical education teachers, personal adult advocates, counselors, social workers, school psychologists, student representatives, food service managers, parent advocates, and health promotion specialists from community agencies. In this new role, the focus of the school is no longer centered only on meeting the daily needs of students. In the new intervention system I am advocating, students will not have to depend solely on school nurses like Lorraine Esper for an adult source of support. They will have many open doors occupied by personal counselors, personal adult advocates, peers, and so on. I argue that this reallocation of helping resources will help shift the school nurse's role from simply reacting to student needs to a major role in prevention and include the following activities:

1. Offering ongoing prevention groups for students, often cofacilitated by school health team members such as counselors to address the key health-risk behaviors identified by the CDC, such as tobacco use, unhealthy eating, inadequate physical activity, alcohol or other drug use, risky sexual behaviors, and destructive behaviors that can lead to injury or even death.
2. Inviting community health and mental health agencies to become partners with the school in a CSPH that offers a variety of medical and health counseling services within the school building during the day and evening as well as serving as sources of referral for students and families with problems related to eating disorders, potential suicide, drug, tobacco, or alcohol addiction, and so on.
3. Utilizing this new partnership with community health and mental health agencies to seek funding that will support a coordinated school health program. For example, the Florida Department of Education, which requires a three-year commitment from schools to work toward establishing a CSHP, provides annual training from a team, technical assistance, and a small grant. CSHP collaborations might also include the sharing of the services of a nurse practitioner between the school and local hospital in order to free the school nurse to carry out CSHP activities.
4. Teaming with other members of the CSHP such as health and physical education teachers, counselors, personal adult advocates, Child Study Team and Kids in Need Committee members, student representatives, food service managers, parent advocates, and health promotion specialists from local health and mental health agencies to affect students' health-related behaviors. At McIntosh Middle School in Sarasota, Florida, the CSHP and the Jewish Family and

Children's Services collaborated to develop a rehabilitation program as an alternative to out-of-school suspensions. The organization provided $15,000 to support professional individual and group counseling for troubled students, mentors from the community to help with their academic work, and greater opportunities for physical safety. The McIntosh CSHP has also teamed with Sarasota Memorial Hospital and utilized the hospital's resources to provide school-based health screening, counseling, health education, and health promotion to the staff as well as fitness and health screening and health education for students.

5. Collaborating with CSHP team members to sell the notion that participation in a daily regimen of physical activity is a contributing factor in increased student achievement. For example, in Illinois 30 percent of the schools have new physical education programs, many of which look like the local health club. As WTTW-Chicago reporter Elizabeth Brackett states, physical education is more than volleyball and competitive sports as in the past.[26] New PE students at Madison Junior High in Naperville, Illinois, spend their forty-minute gym period scaling down walls, running on treadmills, and using weight machines. In addition, screening of area children by Phil Lawler, the district's Physical Education Coordinator, found an astonishing 40 percent had high cholesterol readings.

Dr. Vincient Bufalino, a cardiologist, reviewed the data and found that it was not so much genetics but fast-food restaurant use and lack of exercise that were the two biggest predictors of whether kids had high cholesterol or not. Lawler makes the connection between the value of the daily delivery of physical education and increased academic performance by suggesting that the school finished number one in the Tims test in the world of science and sixth in the world in math. Lawler states, "We truly feel we were a contributing factor to these test scores with the brain research that says physical activity affects the brain." Lawler found support for the new PE movement from Chicago-based Wilson Sporting Goods Company, whose president Jim Baugh says, "You have to condition people. Just like you're teaching kids how to read or write or arithmetic, you have to teach them how to develop an active lifestyle."[27]

According to Brackett, Baugh founded PE for Life, a national advocacy group, to promote funding for daily PE programs across the country. Lawler again makes the political selling point for daily PE when he suggests, "New PE programs must show measurable results just as academic programs are measured by test score results. At Madison, a fitness profile is developed for each student that includes the wearing of heart-rate monitors so teachers and students can measure their effort level. The results are downloaded after class and become a part of the student's fitness profile. The monitors taught me that even slow-moving students may be exercising at their maximum level of effort. Now with this technology we give kids credit for what they do."[28]

Reporter Evelyn Porreca Vuko supports Lawler's observations by citing a study of the California Department of Education's 2001 Physical Fitness Test, which revealed academic achievement is directly associated with quality physical education and that a student's well-being has a direct impact on his or her ability to be successful in school.[29] Vuko also cites the American Academy of Pediatrics' recommendation that children get at least thirty minutes of "moderately strenuous activities" daily.

6. Collaborate with teachers in various academic areas to use health-promotion activities in their curriculum. For example, at Rock Hill High School in North Carolina, the drama class developed material on teen sexuality, the computer class developed an award-winning tobacco use prevention program, the family life classes provide CPR training, the science department addresses how nutrition affects body function, the freshman orientation addresses personal hygiene, and the English classes assign health-related reading and research projects.

7. Serve as an ongoing source of training and referral for staff members as well as offering staff development workshops on staff health issues such as stress reduction, nutrition, eating disorders, drug, alcohol and tobacco abuse, issues related to aging, hypertension, physical activity, and so on so teachers can serve as positive models of health and well-being. As described in *Stories from the Field*, the Bellville Henderson Central School in upstate New York CSHP team organized a one-day staff development workshop at the Beaver Camp Retreat

Center that included all faculty and staff—teachers, bus drivers, secretaries, food service personnel, and health and mental health professionals. The morning session was devoted to team-building activities. In the afternoon session participants met in small groups to discuss how to make the school a better place for adults to work and students to grow. Some of the proposed solutions identified were arranging an early breakfast just for socializing with parents; designing activities that involve parents in the learning process; sharing e-mail addresses with parents; having more days like those spent at Beaver Camp Retreat Center; conducting more mixed group discussions and activities; and providing more guidance for new teachers.

8. Serving as an ongoing source of support and referral for parents on the health issues identified earlier for students and teachers.

9. Playing a leadership role in offering wellness workshops, conferences, and community forums that target specific health and wellness issues, such as obesity.

10. Training and utilizing a cadre of student peer leaders to serve as co-facilitators in helping groups, workshops, and conferences. For example, learning to communicate with peers who may be facing difficult decisions in their lives, visiting elementary schools to assist teachers with health lessons; participating in assemblies that promote positive health choices, and alerting the CSHP of student concerns such as alcohol abuse at Homecoming and proms and during school breaks.

11. Continually looking for new opportunities to promote the health and wellness needs of students and parents. For example, in Chula Vista, California, the school district, city, and the Sharp Chula Vista hospital developed a mobile health clinic to rotate among five schools with high absenteeism, treating problems that would otherwise have kept pupils at home, such as asthma.

According to health and fitness writer Richard Rothstein, the clinic service, which employs a nurse, a nurse practitioner, and a nurse assistant, has helped to bring about an increase in attendance and test scores for many students from low income and non–English-speaking families.[30] Rothstein indicates the success of the program also stems from the clinic's ties to other services. After a pupil has been treated at the clinic, volunteers introduce the child's mother to a family center on school grounds. There, mothers are recruited for English-language classes and a paraprofessional tries to enroll their children in a health plan. Some, whose family income is too high for Medicaid but too low for private coverage, may be eligible for the federally subsidized Children's Health Insurance Program.

Largely because of the efforts of the paraprofessional Aida Meza, three-fourths of the school district's pupils now have health insurance. Most of the rest get free care at the mobile clinic. The family center also provides training for mothers who work as community liaisons throughout Chula Vista. The mothers conduct classes for neighbors on issues like the importance of prenatal care, watching for diabetes, and identifying women in depression. The clinic, the family center, and the school nurse all share a common concern: to keep children healthy enough to attend school and alert enough to do well. These services cost an average of about three hundred dollars per pupil, paid by the participating hospital, San Diego County, the City of Chula Vista, Medicaid, private foundations, and the school district.

According to Rothstein, the program at Chula Vista provides data that early intervention can be successful in providing alternatives to the research finding of Janet Currie of the University of California and Mark Stabile of the University of Toronto that for children whose mothers are not high school graduates, each incidence of serious disease or injury raises the chance of being in the bottom fifth of test scores by 7 percent.

This will certainly require a new kind of thinking on behalf of the principal, school nurse, health educators, and physical education staff. As *Stories from the Field* suggests, when a CSHP succeeds, principals are actively engaged in developing a vision for the program and promoting team activities. They communicate health messages and model healthy behaviors. Principals also communicate the message that the welfare of students is the responsibility of the entire community of which the school is a part. This process requires collaboration and sharing of resources between school and community, involving many agencies and organizations to help address some aspect of a coordinated school health program. An example of the new kind of thinking required on the part of the principal is the understanding that the CSHP approach does not add another administrative layer; it simply confirms the need to manage the components as an organized system. Nor does the approach increase responsibilities of the principal, teachers, and staff; instead, it structures how these responsibilities are addressed.

Therefore, the principal's vision and messages must be broad and include many of the components of a CSHP as clearly defined and equal partners. Here is an example of a vision and message principals might consider. Researcher and author Joy Dryfoos suggests that the health needs of students be addressed through on-site health services including immunization and supported by counselors who are assigned to work closely with students, families, and school staff, a student adult advocate, teachers who incorporate health information into their curriculum, and trained health educators and youth workers from the community who can teach social and behavioral skills.[31] Dryfoos describes some specific models that principals can reflect on in creating a new vision, such as the Children's Aid Society Schools model in which each community school has a built-in primary health center, staffed by a health agency such as Visiting Nurses and the Beacons model, pioneered in New York City through the Department of Youth and Community Development, which picks up where the school system leaves off. Community-based agencies receive grants to go into schools and establish programs such as health centers and drug prevention that are available to neighborhood students and families from early morning until late evening every day throughout the year.

Dryfoos states that these examples all rely on partnerships between school and community agencies. Increasingly, schools in all corners of the United States report formal and informal relationships with outside agencies. A process pioneered by Communities-in-Schools, for example, involves the business community to act as brokers for bringing community services to thousands of school buildings. Hundreds of primary health care clinics are moving into school buildings under the auspices of public and nonprofit community health agencies.

Health education writer Janis Tomlinson suggests that the school-based health centers advocated by Dryfoos are one example of the possible components in coordinated school health programs, centers that combine medical care with preventive and mental health services on the school campus, extending school health services to serve the specific needs of children in the community.[32]

Education writer Darcia Harris-Bowman reports that there are 1,500 school-based health centers nationwide that bring a wide range of medical, nutritional, and mental health care services to millions of students and their families.[33] The centers provide an important safety net for children and adolescents, particularly the more than ten million today that lack health insurance. Harris-Bowman points out that at Broad Acres School in Silver Spring, Maryland, school nurse Ladys Lux is more than a school nurse; she's a lifeline. The school, though located in wealthy Montgomery County, is at the heart of an unofficial village of squat brick apartment buildings isolated from the world around it by class, language, and culture. Inside the buildings, it is typical for two or more families to share a two-bedroom unit, adding to the stress the occupants already face each day as they juggle multiple low-wage jobs in hotels, restaurants, and landscaping and construction companies, work that may be there one day and gone the next.

The school itself has the dubious distinction of being the 140,000-student Montgomery County district's neediest; nearly 94 percent of the 500 pupils receive free or reduced price lunches. Spanish is the dominant language spoken in the community, followed by Vietnamese, and nearly 30 percent of the students are enrolled in remedial English. Broad Acres' student mobility rate hovers around 30 percent. The health center at Broad Acres has the full support of principal Jody Leleck, who is working to raise her school's academic standards in today's world of high-stakes testing. "You can't understand the stress these children suffer in a high-poverty environment," she says, "and the stress manifests itself in so many ways. If we didn't have the health center, my full time job would be social services, and we'd never get to the learning piece."[34]

Yet in a way the students and families at Broad Acres are lucky. They have a number of lifelines, or "open doors" as I call them, at the school called Linkages to Learning. This program has a fourteen-person staff headed up by Maria Conteras, a full-time mental health therapist. The Linkages to Learning staff includes nurse Ladys Lux, nurse practitioner Cara Soifer, a full-time mental health specialist, a part-time psychologist, therapists, social workers, five interns from area universities, and a psychiatrist who comes twice a month to write and adjust prescriptions. Linkages to Learning also offers English-language and computer instruction for parents, seminars on pressing health topics, nutrition counseling for families, and other services. The addition of many of these community and mental health professionals to the Broad Acres setting has taken a great deal of pressure off the school staff who would otherwise deliver the services. As nurse practitioner Cara Soifer reports, "When I first got here I felt I had to ration out the referrals to the school guidance counselor. Now I don't hesitate."[35]

However, *Stories from the Field* wisely warns principals and school health reform advocates that developing the collaboration that is the hallmark of a CSHP is an evolutionary process. Participants need time to develop relationships, understand each other's disciplines, overcome turf issues, and agree on roles. Building the infrastructure for a CSHP is neither easy nor an end in itself. Rather, it is a foundation for a system designed to ensure that students are well enough to learn and ultimately become productive citizens. *Stories from the Field* also warns of the difficult choices involved as a result of funding cuts. The principal of McIntosh Middle School reports, "The biggest challenge has been a reduction in force during the coordinated school health program's duration. Each year we have had to use a different spin for maintenance. Since I never allowed the CSHP to become another layer of accountability with staff, it has survived cuts and rollbacks. You have an obligation to serve students. It won't go away. What students face today is so unwholesome. This model provides hope."

The report also widely includes a warning from a member of the New Tier High School's All-School Wellness Team (ASWT) that, "The more successful a school is, the harder change is. The school community gets very nervous when you change a formula that appears to work. Because of teachers' autonomy, this is not a lock-step institution. Change is more evolutionary. The All-School Wellness Team is making what was once a complex, fragmented system more organized." It replaces what several New Tier staff members described as "a culture of independent contractors," such as school social workers, a schoolwide advisor system in which every student belongs to a group of about twenty-five same sex pupils that meets daily with a classroom teacher who has volunteered to be their advisor, with the goal of preventing students from falling through the cracks, a wellness program for the faculty, and so on. As the report suggests, "We were all over the place. Because we hadn't shared what we were doing, no one realized how programs evolved. It was chaos."

Health education writer Tomlinson addresses other concerns that often take place in building a successful CSHP program. She warns that controversy can follow if the feelings of community members and parents are ignored, for example, their concern that the coordinated school health program is possibly preempting parents in overseeing medical care and counseling for their children, or offering birth control services. Tomlinson also addresses the concern about the lack of preparedness that teachers themselves feel in dealing with health issues. She reports in a recent survey of teachers in Montana's health enhancement program, a program that combines physical education with health education, teachers across the board felt better prepared to teach subjects traditionally identified with physical education, such as team sports or fundamental motor skills. They felt far less ready to teach topics aligned with health education, such as disease prevention or conflict resolution. Tomlinson also raises a question about educators' preparedness to teach health effectively when, she points out, less than 5 percent of health educators in 1994 had majored in health education and almost 37 percent majored in a nonhealth-related field.

Reporter Bonnie Rothman Morris points out the resistance some parents will offer to school districts getting into the business of providing assessment on their children's health in addition to academic progress.[36] For example, in the East Penn School District in Emmaus, Pennsylvania, which has 6,700 students, about 400 parents received a letter from the nurse's office stating that their child was at risk for being overweight. Morris described the angry reactions of some parents, such as Heather Jones, who said, "I took offense to it. I really thought it was inappropriate for school to send a letter." The letter Mrs. Jones received regarding her eighty-five-pound son said the boy's body mass index was in the 85th percentile and was a potential health hazard.

In Citrus County, Florida, the Citrus County Health Department coordinated a plan to place similar letters in children's backpacks. The backlash by parents resulted in a series of meetings where some parents argued that the delivery method could damage the children's self-esteem. Dr. George Ziolkowski, director of Pupil Personnel Services at the East Penn School District, countered by saying he pushed for the notification program after eight East Penn High School nurses noticed weight gains. He said the 400 or so letters represented about 13 percent of the 3,000 students tested so far. Parents of severely underweight children were also notified. None of them complained.

But the incident can serve as a reminder that health promotion messages to parents that are specific to their children need to be carefully executed and seen as supportive. Dr. William Dietz, director of the division of nutrition and physical activity at the Centers for Disease Control and Prevention, noted that the letter might have been better received if it had been phrased differently. He said, "We're in the very early stages of recognition of overweight as a health problem; it's still widely perceived as a cosmetic issue." Dr. Dietz said the letter failed to take the onus off parents. Changes in the way Americans live, including less time in the school day for physical activity, are also partly to blame, he said.

But overall, the biggest obstacle to developing a successful CSHP may be the perception that health education and health promotion have been given secondhand status in our academically oriented large secondary schools. As education reporter Kathy Checkley points out, four out of five parents believe health education is more important than or as important as other school subjects and the majority of adults think that a health content definitely should be included in a kindergarten through twelfth-grade curriculum and include such topics as substance use and abuse and disease prevention and control, and how to maintain mental and emotional health.[37]

However, Checkley reports that according to Becky Smith, executive director of the American Association of Health Educators, despite such strong support from parents and community members, health education has not attained a significant role in schools. Smith contends that many administrators think health education doesn't need much attention, as health information is so prevalent and so readily available. Smith argues that dispensing health information is not health education. She suggests, "Most programs focus on information delivery rather than skills development. The focus, instead, should be on how we help students make decisions with the information they get. And that approach requires teachers who understand what it means to be health-literate and who know what curricula, lessons and instructional strategies help develop literacy in others."

Unfortunately, as Joyce Fetro, associate professor of health education at Southern Illinois University, suggests, "Too often kids come out of school without the skills they need to become productive citizens. They need training in developing personal and social skills such as communication, decision-making and goal setting."[38]

As with the other components in the intervention system I am proposing, a major part of the work in elevating health education and promotion to an equal partnership with academic teachers then rests with the building principal. His or her task is to sell academic teachers on the necessity of including health-related activities in their curriculum, provide them with the training on how to proceed in this task, expect that they adhere to this new role, and use his or her position to argue that health education and promotion is a critical component in the school's curriculum. This selling process on the part of the principal is critical because academic teachers know, as Checkley observes, that health content-related questions do not appear on high-stakes tests and, according to Beverly Bradley, past president of the American School Health Association, "Learning about health hasn't managed to get up there in the hierarchy of importance."

Without the prodding of the principal, academic teachers will continue to say of health education, "Gee, it's really nice; we wish we had time to do it," according to health education consultant Kathleen Middleton. And, according to reporter Christine Davenport, there will be education leaders like John R. Woolums, the director of governmental relations for the Maryland Association of Boards of Education, who argue that students already have many demands on their time and that forcing them to exercise would only cut away time from academics.[39] Woolums states, "We barely have time for English, language arts, math and the core components."

As reported by Checkley, Deborah Haber, associate director of School Health Programs at the Education Development Center in Newton, Massachusetts, has some good advice for principals who are committed to developing a successful CSHP when she recommends, "We need to do a better job of showing teachers how health concepts can be taught in today's classroom, and how to structure activities to deliver skills and content. We need to get better at incorporating what we know about health into everything that's taught, and we need to make it a conscious thing. Students and teachers need to know when they are looking at issues through a health care lens." Haber points out that "health educators could do more to make connections between disciplines obvious. The health educator should be prepared to go to the science or social studies teacher and say, "Let's create a lesson plan that incorporates health concepts and also meets your learning objectives."[40]

But perhaps the best selling model principals can follow for getting opponents such as teachers, administrators, parents, and students advocating for increased time for academics on board as partners in a CSHP can be found in the work of Madison Junior High School Physical Education Coordinator Phil Lawler. As I described earlier in this chapter, Lawler argues that educators who trade gym time for academics are unlikely to get the results they want and that recent brain research shows better brain function after exercise. Lawler is proactive and believes physical education is a contributing factor for the increased test scores and student achievement. He is an advocate who believes in the message that "if we don't teach kids to exercise early, we're not going to get them to do it when they're forty or fifty." Lawler also appears to be well grounded in the political realities of changing a system. Lawler understands that the new PE programs must show measurable results just as academic programs are measured by test score results.

He uses technology to develop a fitness profile to measure each student's progress, a process that not only enables him to teach students the long-term value of daily activity but also sends the message to academic teachers that his version of the new PE is not just fuzzy thinking but is data driven and a contributing factor to their students' academic success and their own success as teachers. This lesson is not lost on high-achieving students and parents looking for a leg up in the competitive world of college admissions and educators and parents looking for new intervention approaches to help marginal students. Lawler also understands that this new version of PE needs external advocates and supporters so he has backup funding. By collaborating with Jim Baugh he has a safety net that provides him with breathing room when budget cuts loom. And his collaboration with Jim Baugh enables him to showcase his work to a national audience. The Naperville district is now the showcase for Baugh's PE for Life site.

In the end, creating an intervention system that includes the integration of many components—personal counselors for individual and group counseling and training; teachers as personal adult advocates; students, support staff, and parents as sources of help and support on the frontlines of the school; and enhancing the role of the school nurse with the creation of a collaborated school health program—involves the principal playing many roles. He or she must be a visionary, listener, salesperson, politician, collaborator, facilitator, confronter, supporter, and prodder who delivers affirmation as well as helpful criticism each day. But I believe his or her most important role is to model the helping process and demonstrate that he or she genuinely cares about the well-being of his or her students, staff, parents, and himself or herself.

A principal must look close, as it is the closer look that gets at the problem, to listen and not turn a blind eye to troubled students. It is by truly listening to students' stories that we arrive at providing the open doors for help that fit them and their needs. Nurse practitioner Cara Soifer at Broad Acres School zeroes in on our need to listen when she describes some of her students as "frequent fliers," meaning students who show up at counseling and health centers on a daily basis. These are students who tend to trot in regularly with vague complaints and symptoms, students who are troubled with personal and/or health and well-being problems in school and/or at home but are not yet ready to share their stories, not sure if this is the right place, a safe area of comfort and support, to ask for help. These are the kinds of students who need extra time to begin talking about what is really going on with them.

In a sense the relationship between Cara Soifer and her students is not unlike an effective doctor–patient relationship in which the helper sets the stage for open communication. However, as Dr. Wendy Levinson, vice chairwoman of the University of Toronto's Department of Medicine, indicates, when patients' complaints are ignored, or their expression is interrupted, there is an increased likelihood that they will reemerge just when the visit is ending. Patients need time to talk and feel they are listened to and have the doctor's full attention.[41]

And so do students. Effective school helpers, like good doctors, listen carefully, ask open-ended questions, make eye contact, and indicate they care. As reporter Meredith Levine suggests, good doctors do not pepper patients with questions. There is a clear connection between positive doctor–patient relationships and improvements in the patient's health. The same might be said of positive helper–student relationships. Levine also points out that in an organization where doctors were unhappy, they tended to have more problematic communication with their patients. This, too, can be said of helpers working in settings in which their value and expertise are not affirmed. What works to help students improve their worth and well-being also works the same for professionals and support staff.

In the next chapter, I present a case study of how one high school built an effective intervention that was able to respond to a variety of student and parent problems. It was an intervention system that became more effective because of a crisis involving acting-out students, angry peers, disappointed parents and educators, and administrators who felt the wrath from parents and community members when they acted, some said, too hastily. This crisis also presented me with the opportunity to use my counseling, training, and program development skills to fill a much-needed role in the school's intervention system, become an integral and valued member of the school's helping team, and educate parents and community members to the hard truth that any student, even the best and brightest, is capable of heading toward the margins of school life.

NOTES

1. National Association of Secondary School Principals (NASSP), *Executive Summary of Breaking Ranks 11: Strategies for Leading High School Reform* (Reston, Va.: NASSP, 2004), 1–6.

2. Carla Smith, "A Model of Leadership," National Association of Secondary School Principals (NASSP), principals.org, January 2004; www.nassp.org/publications/plpl_model_leadership_0104.cfm (accessed 13 January 2004).

3. Marge Scherer, "Perspectives: Connected at the Roots," *Educational Leadership 61*(9) (May 2004); www.ascd.org/publications/ed_lead/200405/scherer.html (accessed 6 April 2004).

4. Pedro A. Noguera, "Special Topics: Transforming High School," *Educational Leadership 61*(9) (May 2004); www.ascd.org/publications/edlead/200405/noguera.html (accessed 6 April 2004).

5. Michael Erard, "Where to Get a Good Idea: Steal It Outside Your Group," newyorktimes.com, May 2004; www.newyorktimes.com/200405/arts/22IDEA.html (accessed 28 May 2004).

6. Robert Hampel, *The Last Citadel* (Boston: Houghton Mifflin, 1986), 7–8, 51–53.

7. Harold Munson, "Guidance in Secondary Education: Reconnaissance and Renewal," in *Guidance for Education in Revolution*, ed. David R. Cook (Boston: Allyn & Bacon, 1971), 179.

8. Arthur G. Powell, Eleanor Farrar, and David Cohen, *The Shopping Mall High School* (Boston: Houghton Mifflin, 1985), 8–9, 34–37, 86, 91, 268–269, 318.

9. David R. Cook, "The Future of Guidance as a Profession," in *Guidance for Education in Revolution*, ed. David R. Cook (Boston: Houghton Mifflin, 1971), 517, 524, 529-31, 548.

10. Gregg Winter, "Wooing the Counselor Raises Enrollments and Also Eyebrows," *New York Times*, July 8, 2004, pp. 1, 18 (A).

11. Shelly Reese, "The Counselor's Conundrum: Provide Triage or Full-Service Programs," *Middle Ground* (October 1998): 17–19, 24.

12. Sachem (NY) North High School, "Guidance," Sachem North High School website, 2003–2004; www.sachem.edu/schools/north/guidance2003_2004/index/html (accessed 26 February 2004).

13. American School Counselor Association (ASCA), *Executive Summary of the ASCA National Model: A Framework for School Counseling Programs* (Alexandria, Va.: American School Counselor Association, 2002), 1.

14. Judy L. Bowers, and Patricia A. Hatch, *The ASCA National Model for School Counseling Programs*, (Alexandria, Va.: American School Counselor Association, 2002), 7–9.

15. Judy L. Bowers, and Patricia A. Hatch, *The ASCA National Model for School Counseling Programs*.

16. Philip Walter, "Schools Say Counseling Efforts Are Improving," *The Virginian-Pilot*, September 18, 1996, pp. 1, 9 (A).

17. Joetta L. Stack, "Riley Says It's Time to Rethink High Schools," *Education Week*, September 22, 1999, p. 20.

18. Association for Supervision and Curriculum Development (ASCD), "The Counselor's Role," *ASCD Curriculum Update*, Fall 1999.

19. Association for Supervision and Curriculum Development (ASCD), "Schools as Communities," *ASCD Curriculum Update*, Fall 1999.

20. Richard Scardamaglia, "Teachers as Student Advocates," *Educational Leadership 50*(4) (December 1992–January 1993): 31–33.

21. Pedro A. Noguera, "Special Topics: Transforming High Schools," *Educational Leadership 61*(9) (April 2004); www.ascd.org/publications/edlead/200405/noguera.html (accessed 6 May 2004).

22. Bonnie Bernard, "Fostering Resiliency in Kids," *Educational Leadership 51*(3) (November 1993); www.ascd.org/readingroom/edlead/9311/bernard.html (accessed 7 June 2002).

23. Shelly Reese, "The Counselor's Conundrum: Provide Triage or Full-Service Programs."

24. Elizabeth Austin, "Profile of Lisa Berkman," *Advances 3*. Princeton, N.J.: Robert Wood Johnson Foundation, (2000): 4.

25. Centers for Disease Control and Prevention (CDC), *Stories from the Field: Lessons Learned about Building Coordinated School Health Programs* (Atlanta: Centers for Disease Control and Prevention, 2003), xiv, 1–5, 25–26, 42, 45–46, 54, 72, 81.

26. Elizabeth Brackett, "Fit for Life," PBS Interview, March 22, 2002; www.pbs.org/newshour/bb/education/jan-june-2/pc_3-22.html (accessed 27 March 2002).

27. Elizabeth Brackett, "Fit for Life."

28. Elizabeth Brackett, "Fit for Life."

29. Evelyn Porreca Vuko, "Youth Movement: How to Put Exercise into Play," washingtonpost.com, 23 December 2003, p. c10; www.washingtonpost.com/ac2/wp-dyn/A23125-2003Ced22?language=printer (accessed 11 March 2004).

30. Richard Rothstein, "A Mobile Clinic Delivers Good Health and Grades," *New York Times*, 11 September 2002, p. 8 (B).

31. Joy Dryfoos, "The Mind-Body Building Equation," *Educational Leadership* 57(6) (March 2000); www.ascd.org/readingroom/edlead.0003/dryfoos.html (accessed 7 April 2002).

32. Janis Tomlinson, "A Changing Panorama," Association for Supervision and Curriculum Development (ASCD), *Infobrief* 27 (May 1999); www.ascd.org/readingroom/infobrief/9905.html (accessed 7 April 2002).

33. Darcia Harris-Bowman, "Health-Care Hub," *Education Week*, February 4, 2004; http://edweek.org/ew_printstory.cfm?slug-21HealthCenter.h23 (accessed 2 June 2004).

34. Darcia Harris-Bowman, "Health-Care Hub."

35. Darcia Harris-Bowman, "Health-Care Hub."

36. Bonnie Rothman Morris, "Letters on Students' Weight Ruffle Parents," *New York Times*, March 26, 2002, p. 7 (F).

37. Kathy Checkley, "Emphasizing Skills and Prevention to Form a More Health-Literate People," Association for Supervision and Curriculum Development (ASCD), *Health Education Curriculum Update* (Spring 2000); www.ascd.org/readingroom/cupdate/2000/lspring00.html (accessed 7 April 2002).

38. Kathy Checkley, "Emphasizing Skills and Prevention to Form a More Health-Literate People."

39. Christine Davenport, "Student Obesity Targeted," washingtonpost.com, February 11, 2004, p. BO5; www.washingtonpost.som/ac2/wp-dyn/A30235-2004Feb10?language=printer (accessed 11 March 2004).

40. Kathy Checkley, "Emphasizing Skills and Prevention to Form a More Health-Literate People."

41. Meredith Levine, "Tell the Doctor All Your Problems But Keep It to Less Than a Minute," *New York Times*, June 1, 2004, p. 6 (F).

4

How a Crisis Spurred an
Intervention System at One High School

Building a clear, practical, systematic intervention system to promote the health and well-being of young people so that their physical, emotional, and social problems do not interfere with student functioning and so they may learn to practice healthy behaviors and become productive citizens is an evolutionary process. This process is often sparked by an incident involving students in a number of the Center for Disease Control and Prevention's (CDC) key health-risk behaviors, such as tobacco use, unhealthy eating, inadequate physical activity, alcohol and drug use, sexual behaviors that result in infection and unintended pregnancies, and behaviors that result in violence and unintentional injury or even death.[1] This process shakes up the status quo and the school–community feeling that all is well among our students.

Such was the case at Shoreham-Wading River High School in the late 1980s and early 1990s. As I briefly described in an earlier publication,[2] the prevailing wisdom at that time among staff in the Shoreham-Wading River School District and parents in the adjoining Shoreham and Wading River communities, located in eastern Long Island, was that they were blessed with ample funding from the nuclear power plant being built in the district and that because of the many open doors for help available, students would not end up heading toward the margins of school life. It was felt that this combination of ample resources, a young and dedicated staff, and parent involvement and support would somehow spare their children from the health risks identified by the CDC. That was not to be the case. As the Shoreham students moved from the seeming safety of their elementary and middle school experiences into the high school setting, they, like many teenagers, encountered troubles with relationships, family life, academic failure, poor health habits and growing addictions to tobacco, alcohol, and drugs, eating disorders, and so on.

They had more open doors for help than many other schools, in the form of three guidance counselors, a school psychologist, a part-time social worker, an exemplary school nurse, an advisory system called House Groups, in which teachers acted as advisors and personal adult advocates for ten to twelve students of the same grade level, a new approach to physical education similar to Phil Lawler's new program, a leadership class offered as a regular part of the curriculum to a select group of eleventh-grade students, an alternative school housed within the high school that served approximately twenty underachieving students, a Child Study Team (CST), and a Kids in Need (KIN) Committee. The school and the leadership provided by district superintendent Richard Doremus and high school principal Norman Bussiere had already implemented many of the recommendations of the *Breaking Ranks 11* report, some of the components of a comprehensive school health program (CSHP), and some of the intervention components I have advocated for in this book.

But the high school intervention system had both external and internal problems. Externally, the school had a perception problem with some educators, parents, and community members outside the school setting. The high school often found its strengths and contributions dwarfed in comparison to the Shoreham-Wading River Middle School, which was receiving national attention for its advisory system and student-centered programs. The middle school, a model for the reforms advocated in the 1989 report *Turning Points: Preparing American Youth for the 21st Century*, was overwhelmed by visiting educators from schools throughout the country, even international educators, and its administrators and staff were invited to serve as keynote speakers at national conferences and contribute their observations in writing to middle-level journals and textbook seminars.[3] Nationally, the middle schools were being heralded as the model to pursue for secondary education while critics of high schools increased their assaults, backed up by the *A Nation at Risk* report that called for ways to increase the achievement of high school students[4] and books such as *The Shopping Mall High School*, which described the abrogation of authority by teachers and the increasing violence and acting-out behaviors of students.[5]

It clearly was a pro-middle school period. This national criticism of high schools was felt at the local level in Shoreham where some of the members of the school district staff, parents, and community viewed the high school as the one district school housing troubled students, students who were out of step with the sought-after image of Shoreham students being healthy, well-behaved, athletic, and high achievers. What was missing in these critics' analyses was the understanding that high school students indeed tend to act out more and not go quietly as they head toward the margins.

As the reader knows, big kids sometimes have big problems. Many of the complex problems of adolescents do not have simple solutions. And many educators, parents, and community members looking at the culture of high schools are angry at troubled teens and are prone to cast blame for these students' behaviors on the high school staff and organization.

In my observations, students headed toward the margins at the high school were often viewed as misfits who were ungrateful for their wonderful education and supportive parents and community and selfishly throwing away the healthy behaviors and lessons learned in earlier grades. Literally, they were seen as destroying their opportunities for college and the good life by drifting into acting-out behaviors, academic failure, addictions, poor health habits, and destructive relationships.

This negative perception of teenagers, I believe, is not peculiar to the Shoreham and Wading River communities. Data from the Public Agenda study "Kids These Days: What Americans Really Think about the Next Generation" echoes this point of view.[6] The study states that for many adults teen behavior is more than disappointing, it can be intimidating. When asked what comes first to their minds when they think about today's teenagers, two-thirds (67 percent) immediately reach for negative adjectives such as rude, irresponsible, and wild. In the study there were few complimentary comments about teenagers. Only a handful (12 percent) describe teens positively, using terms like smart or helpful. Adults in the study also reported that it is very common for teenagers to get into trouble because they have too much free time. Four in ten Americans (46 percent) said it's very common to find teenagers who have poor work habits and lack self-discipline. Even the people who have regular contact with

teens are as critical as everyone else, if not more so. Two-thirds (65 percent) of those with a lot of contact describe teenagers disapprovingly.
Even parents have a negative view of teens. Only 12 percent said teens are
friendly and helpful and only 9 percent said teens treat people with respect.

In a sense, the Shoreham-Wading River High School, like many high
schools, was an island in which educators were trying to address the growing personal and well-being problems of students that were emerging in the
1980s and 1990s but in that effort they found themselves out of step with
the seeming orderliness, tidiness, and quietness of younger students in
other district schools. High schools like Shoreham can be messy places
with staff continuously facing a variety of student problems, sometimes
emerging all at once and overwhelming the schools' supposedly efficient
intervention system. And more often than not, the staff in schools like
Shoreham High, even in amply supported school districts, are relegated to
a stepchild role of dealing with the pressured and unpredictable world of
adolescents and left with little time for self-promotion activities such as
winning awards, becoming convention keynoters and taking on a role of
scholar/author, speaking and writing on education reform—activities that
could serve as political cover and protection from critics who view
teenagers as trouble and troubled.

But Shoreham-Wading River High School also had organizational and
training problems with its loosely connected intervention system. For example, the three counselors were locked in a quasi-administrative role in
which they were assigned to students by alphabet and were focused on
college admissions and scheduling, leaving little time for personal counseling and intervention. The school's advisors received little training in
how to interact with advisees and effectively use the advisory time set
aside each morning to enlist students in helpful conversations. Lorraine
Esper, the school nurse, felt she was spending much of her time with "frequent flyer" students and was not called upon to take a more proactive
prevention role as advocated in the coordinated school health programs.

The school psychologist, a very skilled one-on-one counselor, found
much of his time taken up with chairing the CST and KIN committees and
preparing individual education plans for the increasing number of special
education students flocking into the district. The parent training that was
sporadically available through the PTA served to speak only to the con-

verted. The hard-to-reach parents described in the *Breaking Ranks 11* report were left on the sidelines and viewed by parent cliques as not caring and disinterested in their own children's lives.[7] Many of these disenfranchised parents were among a minority of parents who were from the lower class and outside the middle-class culture of the Shoreham-Wading River highly professional community. Finally, some of the students in the alternative school were unable to find a path to succeed even with the small group instruction and nurturing provided by two caring teachers. As a result, many of the supposedly open doors to help for students and parents had limited availability because of the constraints of time, as in the case of the school psychologist, social worker, and nurse; the lack of personal one-on-one and group counseling to address students' key health risks; the lack of ongoing training for advisors; the lack of a mechanism to involve hard-to-reach parents; and a process to collaborate with community agencies that could provide additional helping and educational resources, such as training for GED for underachieving students, treatment for students with addictions or eating disorders, and so on.

Upon reflection, the intervention at Shoreham-Wading River High School was not perfect in spite of the many components in place to serve students and parents. For example, the intervention system needed a proactive plan that included addressing and changing the negative feelings and perceptions of critics that many high school students are troubled and trouble. Such a plan would also promote and sell the notion that the high school had a dedicated, caring, and skilled staff who were committed to providing many open doors for help for students and parents. As in all high schools, critics in Shoreham needed to be addressed, have their issues heard, and be won over as allies whenever possible. Among those critics were many newcomers, parents who had moved to Shoreham for the seeming safety of small town life and the quality of the public schools.

Many of these newcomers were successful professionals involved in education, law enforcement officials, scientists at nearby Brookhaven National Laboratory, and medical professionals from Central Suffolk and Mather Memorial Hospitals. They had moved to Shoreham to escape from the increasing crime and violence in their old neighborhoods. They believed they had found a safe haven where their children could avoid the problems of alcohol, drug and tobacco abuse, eating disorders, sexual diseases, idleness and hanging out, and other risky behaviors. But as the reader knows, many teens have problems and head toward the margins in spite of the seemingly protective blanket that parents try to place over them.

Sometimes the most marginal students are the ones who have been overprotected, coddled, and controlled by parents with good intentions. There needed to be a plan to educate critics, particularly parents, about the issues and problems that can emerge in adolescent life and use this understanding that some teenagers will make mistakes as they face the difficult choices involved in making the transition to adult life, not to view teens who appear and act different as problems and troubled and force them into seeking support and solace from each other, avoiding adult contact. This process encourages isolation, hanging out and using alcohol, drugs, and tobacco, and high-speed car races to find meaning in their lives.

This educative plan also had to involve convincing parents and community members that in spite of all the helping resources at the high school and the skills and good intentions of staff, there was no guarantee that the staff could prevent every student from trouble, even the best and the brightest academic, athletic, and artistic stars. Students like likeable and athletic Calvin Kohart and beloved teachers like Cliff Lennon are going to meet a tragic death on occasion. Some problems and losses are not preventable.

But a caring and supportive school community can help students, parents, and community members learn the skills they will need to face the next round of problems and losses that are sure to come. The crisis that emerged at Shoreham-Wading River High School in the late 1980s brought home the notion that maybe some parents, community members, and educators had not been looking closely at the troubles some seemingly problem-free and well-behaved students were having and that perhaps the school community had been turning a blind eye to the so-called successful students who were heading toward trouble and were too focused on acting-out students.

There seemed to be no immediate need to increase the quality and quantity of individual and group counseling, training for advisors, parent education and involvement, and collaboration with community health and mental health agencies. The school was still young, having been founded in 1973, had a young and energetic staff, many with doctoral degrees, and enjoyed more successes than failures. What was in place perhaps wasn't perfect but things seemed to be working well, for now. As I have suggested early on in this chapter, the process of setting in place the various components in an effective intervention system is evolutionary. Building the infrastructure for an effective intervention system is neither easy nor an end in itself. Critics abound. Rather, it is a foundation for a system designed to ensure that students are well enough to learn and ultimately become productive citizens. As with any system an effective intervention program requires ongoing maintenance and adjustments as it grows and evolves.

More often than not this adjustment process begins with a crisis that involves students acting out and participation in key health-risk behaviors identified by the CDC, a crisis that can bring needed change and integration of an intervention program in which the components are too loosely connected and not poised for team intervention.

In the late 1980s Shoreham-Wading River High School had such a crisis. The reader should keep in mind that the idea of high schools addressing the CDC health-risk areas suggested in *Stories from the Field* was just beginning to gain national attention in the late 1980s. As education consultant Floretta Dukes McKenzie and Julius B. Richmond, MD, professor emeritus at Harvard Medical School, suggest, the concept of school health programs has evolved over the past several decades.[8] In the beginning, discussions of school health focused on curriculum. In 1987, the field took a quantum leap when Diane Allenworth and Lloyd Kolbe described an eight-component model of a comprehensive school health program. It is no surprise, then, that at Shoreham-Wading River High School in 1988, while many students were engaging in risky behaviors with alcohol, drugs, tobacco, eating disorders, and the like, educators, like parents and community members, had not made intervention in these areas a priority. School-related activities in which students abused alcohol were a problem about to happen.

Before I describe the crisis I need to share with the reader the role I had played as an educator in Shoreham up to the crisis and how this episode dramatically changed my role. I had come to the middle school in the early 1980s and was given carte blanche by the principal to expand the personal counseling services for students, training for advisors involved in the school's advisory system, training for support staff, and training for parents on adolescent issues. For me the experience was akin to being a kid in a candy store, free to develop a helping service for a variety of clients, with no constraints.

In a real sense I was experimenting with how to build the various components that go into an effective schoolwide intervention system and how to intervene to help students who were beginning to develop risky health behaviors identified by the CDC. By the mid-1980s, I had developed an evening counseling program for parents; a training program for advisors with the school psychologist; intervention groups for students in such areas as divorce, grieving, and drug and alcohol abuse; parent and support staff training; and a summer wellness program with a physical education teacher for students who were identified as having problems with health issues such as being overweight, low self-esteem, peer relationships, and family problems. Although I didn't realize it at the time, upon reflection I can see that I was getting important experience and training that would serve me when I moved to the high school as a counselor in the late 1980s.

My move to the high school was not of my choosing. In the mid-1980s the then New York State Governor Mario Cuomo announced that he planned to shut down the Shoreham Nuclear Power Plant, from which the school district received the majority of its funding. Having been involved in other school districts that experienced reductions in funding, I had some expertise in seeking funds from foundations and became involved with the superintendent in meeting with heads of foundations in New York City.

I believed we had to mobilize our efforts to seek alternate funding, and fast. As part of that process I developed a new concept for the school as a laboratory for innovations in curriculum, counseling, community service, training advisors, educating parents, and so forth. The plan included creating a teacher training and professional development center for staff where visiting educators as well could gain experience in advising skills, a Saturday Arts and Technology program, a laboratory school for parents, an early morning and after-school health and recreation program for students, and a special wing in the school where faculty, students, and parents would explore new ideas. Foundation funding supported these innovations, which could be studied by educators from throughout the country. But as I saw it, my continued involvement with the superintendent and my authoring of a plan to change the school was not welcomed by the school principal who, while at first supportive, grew more and more resistant and eventually viewed me as a threat, not an ally.

When I asked him for feedback, he suggested it would be better if I moved to the high school, where there was a counseling position open due to a retirement. Upon reflection, this should not have come as a surprise to me. As one New Tier faculty member observed in *Stories from the Field*, "The more successful a school is, the harder the change." I had stepped out of the role of counselor and moved into a leadership role, hoping to be part of the effort to help guide the school through the coming tough times. However, my actions were not welcomed by the principal, who I now believe saw me as being in a competitive, not subservient, role. In reality I had no desire to be an administrator but simply wanted to be a player in this rapidly changing school environment. The result was that one of us would have to go. And that someone was going to be me. My days at the middle school were numbered.

In the leaving process I, like many other education reformers, wondered if I should have played it safer, stayed secure in my counseling role and not become an ally of the superintendent and an advocate for the change that I saw as necessary, given the anticipated huge reductions in funding. I had endless conversations with my wife, colleagues, and myself about the wisdom of the path I had chosen. Was I, like some of the students I counseled, moving toward the margins of my career?

What I didn't realize at the time was that I was ready to move on. It was time. And when the time comes to move on, whether it is in a personal or a professional relationship, it's never easy. It's never the right time to leave. There is no denying that mixed feelings, regrets, and wondering what might have been often overshadow the opportunities that come with closing one door and opening another. But the reality was that I had accomplished my work at the middle school, learned a great deal, and needed a new arena to use my skills, not only as a counselor but also as a leader and team member, a place where I could be valued for my ideas, risk-taking behaviors, and commitment to students, parents, and colleagues.

I didn't realize that my experience at the middle school—offering personal counseling and training; educating and selling staff, parents, community members, and students on the value of such an intervention system and how their helping skills contribute to the system's effectiveness; and

learning to navigate through the politics of resistance to new programs—
helped me to be ready and set to intervene when the crisis occurred in May
1988.

In addition to my new skills, I took with me on my journey to the high
school my observations of many middle school parents that they were
fearful of their children moving on to the high school, where they would
no longer be in the safe cocoon offered at the middle school, on their own
and vulnerable to the pressures of peers to drink and use drugs. Horror stories abounded about high school students' partying. Clearly the high
school was a place that many parents saw as trouble. I was moving from
a school that most parents loved to a school environment that made many
parents uneasy. I hoped would find my niche there.

When I moved to the high school as a counselor and began searching
for ways to expand the guidance office's personal counseling and training
services beyond the traditional counselor role of scheduling and college
advisement, I initially met a dead end. I was advised, one might say
warned, by one of the counselors (who eventually became a supportive
colleague) not to start "your group and middle school huggy-feely stuff
here." The message was, maybe you have great personal counseling and
training skills, but this is a traditional guidance office. We don't do
groups, deep personal counseling, or advisor training. Stick to the scheduling and college advisement and only if that stuff is covered can you do
your little group work and middle school counseling stuff. But that's not
the priority here. Get on the computer and start learning about college
searches. I thought, "Where have I landed and why?"

But the kind of resistance to the personal counseling and training skills
that I could offer at the high school changed with the senior class trip in
May 1988. On the trip it was reported that many seniors had used and
abused alcohol and damaged and vandalized hotel rooms, and the faculty
advisors had condoned or ignored this behavior. Some students even reported that the faculty chaperones encouraged such behavior and joined in
drinking with students. Rumors abounded.

As graduation approached, the administration made a decision that
some of the students identified as leaders in this episode would not be able
to attend their graduation ceremony. Many of these students were high
achievers and athletes with no previous school problems. Of course, many
members of the senior class and their parents reacted to the decision with

anger and outrage and even disbelief. Some questioned where the effort was to help these students reflect on their poor judgment and gain some positive lesson from this sad experience. Their anger spilled over with one parent I knew stating, "It's fine for the school district to preach that they are student centered, but when kids act out who have no previous behavior problems, the school officials cut and run to cover themselves."

But there were educators, parents, and even students in the high school community who countered with the argument that this ill-fated senior trip was in fact a long overdue wake-up call, an opportunity to develop ways to address an ongoing pattern of teens abusing alcohol and drugs at parties on weekends, high-speed car races, and hushed-up overdoses that ended up with students being hospitalized and some sent into rehab. These risky behaviors involved students from every social group—the high achievers and athletes as well as marginal students who were failing. Their point of view was supported by the principal and a group of district educators who were backing a plan to add a student assistance counselor to provide additional counseling and education interventions to help students make more healthy decisions about drugs and alcohol as well as other key health-risk behaviors. If the high school was interested in developing a comprehensive wellness program, it had to go beyond the education provided in health and physical education programs and begin to offer early intervention for students, training for advisors, and education and training for parents.

In June 1988 I suddenly found myself in the right place at the right time. The student assistance counselor position was a wonderful opportunity for me to use my counseling, training, and program development skills. I approached the principal, Norman Bussiere, and laid out a tentative plan for how I could be an asset to aid him and other members of the helping team. For example, I could help the overburdened school psychologist by teaming with him to share counseling loads; team with the school nurse to lead health-related intervention groups; team with teachers in the alternative school to increase their graduation possibilities; team with the peer counseling and leadership class teacher to train students; offer ongoing workshops and forums for parents and community members on the issues involved in adolescent health development and the need for adult mentors to help teenagers navigate through the many personal and education choices they are facing; serve as a trainer for advisors and members of the advisory

committee; serve as a liaison to the health and physical education programs; be a member of the CST and KIN; and finally, be a team member
of the guidance and counseling department.

I also suggested that the student assistance position be a part of, not separate from and in competition with, the three guidance counselors. I knew
from experience that in most schools, when a student assistance counselor
position was added, it was usually a part-time position that was not supported by guidance counselors, who saw the position as a separate agency
that was in direct competition for funding and resources and, as such, a
threat to their survival. My argument was that what I would be doing was
adding another component to the guidance services and to the school's intervention system. I was not going to be a threat. I would be an equal partner with the counselors. They would be able to do what they did best,
which was advising students on course selection, college admissions, and
career choices. I would be providing the personal counseling and training
component.

I also recommended that the student assistance counselor's office be located in close proximity to the guidance, school nurse, and school psychologist's offices, which would enable me to easily team with these professionals, and where I could easily interact with students. My sales pitch
to the principal was that I could add an important piece to the many individual components already in place, which would help take the load off
overburdened team members such as the school nurse and psychologist
and increase the flow of information about students headed toward the
margins and help lead to a coordinated intervention effort.

I was no stranger to the need for this kind of teaming and collaboration
nor to the thinking of progressive educators like Howard Adelman, cofounder of the School Mental Health Project at the University of California at Los Angeles, who suggest personnel providing counseling, psychological, health, and social services in schools need to coordinate with each
other and work toward integration activities.[9] They also need to collaborate with personnel who represent the other components of a coordinated
school health program. Opportunities for collaboration arise daily. For example, a school social worker can advise the school nurse about family
problems that interfere with a student's receiving needed medical care. A
school psychologist can review the mental health unit of a health education curriculum or teach conflict resolution skills to a health class. The

school counselor can consult with the physical educator about a student who cuts class because she is embarrassed to change clothes in the locker room.

Some stories have a happy ending. The principal indicated that he felt my skills were exactly what were needed. Politically, he could now state to the school community that he was taking action to increase the quantity and quality of counseling help for students and parents. And in Bill Fibkins he had a professional who had counseled many of the high school students and parents while in the middle school and was known to the school community, not an outsider who might need years to implement this new program. To shore up my own skills in alcohol and drug counseling, we both agreed that I spend time in July in training at the Hazelden Foundation in Center City, Minnesota. In the meantime, Norman would oversee building an office that was located between the school nurse and guidance offices.

One of the lessons I learned in this 1988 period was that the work of educators like myself, who are interested in reform, involves setbacks and detours. During these bouts of seeming failure, we have to retain the will to win and believe that opportunity will emerge again. We have to believe that we have something valuable to offer our colleagues, students, and parents and we can be useful in helping them meet new challenges. That requires a solid support group when doubts and setbacks arise. For me, the core of that support group was my wife, Kathy, who kept telling me my work at the middle school was done and, like it or not, it was time to close that door. Not all stories end well but there are valuable lessons to be learned. Our experience can serve as a model for students and educators who face personal and professional setbacks.

The Hazelden experience was valuable for me, and many of the facilitators and visiting counselors supported my vision for the student assistance model to offer a variety of the personal counseling and training programs for students, staff, and parents. The experience also taught me that many of the counselors were involved in similar crisis situations in their schools and looking for concrete ways to address the growing personal and well-being needs of students and parents. Upon returning from Hazelden, I knew my first step was to meet with members of the intervention team and ask their input on how to proceed. However, I wanted these conversations to be two way and planned to suggest the kinds of programs I was ready to offer on my own and in partnership with them. I knew this first stage would require that I be very visible, out among the people, so to speak, and be in a selling mode in order to get the various members of the team receptive to what I had to offer to support their efforts.

My first conversations were with the principal, Norman Bussiere. These conversations were an eye-opener for me because, although I had previously talked with him about a variety of outreach programs to students and parents, he was completely focused on getting rid of the alcohol problem in the school. The aftermath of the senior trip was still very much on his mind and it was hard for him to hear about other interventions. He talked abut having assemblies featuring speakers such as recovering alcoholics and victims of drunk drivers, speaker who could share their horror stories about the problems that often arise with alcohol addiction. I pointed out that I felt assemblies might be helpful but first I had to gain trust with students and offer counseling that would respond to a number of problems they were experiencing.

Alcohol abuse was usually accompanied by other personal and health problems. A forty-five-minute assembly probably wasn't going to change student behaviors. But I understood his position and the politics involved in the need to show that the school was responding to the problem. Leaving his office I knew I had to move fast to demonstrate that the counseling service I was about to offer was the best way to proceed to help students who were using and abusing alcohol. And somehow I had to hold at bay the first impulse of some educators, parents, and community members that sermonizing to students about the horrors of addictions at assemblies was the way to proceed. I had to convince people that the way to go was first listening to students, gaining their trust, and involving them in the counseling/educative process of making better choices about their health and well-being and being of support for peers headed for trouble. I didn't have the luxury of time on my side.

Next I met with school psychologist, Ray McGagli. Ray had been at the school since the beginning and was widely respected as a crisis counselor and leader of both the CST and KIN Committee. He was also involved with designing educational plans for the growing number of special education students. Ray was the go-to person when any problems emerged with students and parents. He appeared thrilled that I was coming aboard and would be able to share some of his growing counseling load and be able to offer group intervention, which he had no time to do.

He indicated that he was in over his head trying to handle the evaluations for special education students, meet with parents, facilitate the CST and KIN meetings, and keep up with the growing counseling needs of students. He needed help himself and he saw me as a major source of that help. While I had known many students in the middle school, these kids were different. The students had become teenagers and were no longer little kids with little problems. Ray advised me not to expect a warm reaction from students. I was a face from the past but he suggested that I go about the task of getting to know them, and their parents, as they were now—their problems, hopes, and dreams. He also advised that I conduct a steady outreach to the professional and support staff as well. I was the new kid on the block, not a known quantity. What services could I deliver and how would it support their efforts? Many members of the school community had little idea of my mission and how I was going to proceed, except for a short statement from the principal. Ray also provided me with a list of students and parents who he felt could use my early intervention and would be receptive to my help.

I received the same kind of warm reception from the school nurse, Lorraine Esper, and another dose of practical advice. Lorraine suggested that I move fast to get to know students but also not be seen as the "alcohol counselor" who was hired to stamp out student drinking. She reported that many students were still angry about what they saw as a heavy-handed reaction by the school administration in not letting some students attend their graduation ceremony. Lorraine pointed out that I was in a tough spot. On the one hand I needed the support of the administration, but I had to avoid being seen as their tool. However, Lorraine reassured me that there were plenty of students with problems and anything I could do to help carry the load now being carried by her and Ray McGagli would be appreciated. She, too, provided me with a list of students and parents who needed intervention for a variety of problems, including divorce, abuse, failure, school pressures, and addiction to tobacco.

Lorraine was particularly interested in cofacilitating health-related groups with me, such as how to stop or reduce smoking during the school day, stay sober on the weekends, and get help for eating disorders. She felt that the school needed to address the negative impact of partying on weekends, the growing number of students from every group in the school who were using tobacco, and female students who were into being thin and bordering on becoming anorexic or bulimic.

My conversation with the guidance counselors, Jim Sheridan, Kelley Young, and Sue Ireland, was also helpful. Fortunately I had worked closely with the counselors during the 1987–1988 school year and after an initial "You better do what is expected here" attitude from Jim, we grew to respect each other and value each other's skills. I found this team to be highly effective in advising students and handling all the complicated issues involved in helping students select courses and colleges and meet graduation requirements. On paper, the school's advisors were supposed to help students make most of these choices, but in reality the counselors met with each student to make sure they were on track.

That year in the guidance office taught me the value of their work to students, parents, and advisors and made me very appreciative of their skills. In our meetings the counselors expressed relief that now they might be able to begin to avoid the constant criticism from parents, advisors, and some students that they were not doing enough to help troubled students. They were sick of being scapegoats. My appointment as the student assistance counselor who was a member of the guidance and counseling team provided them with necessary political cover. And they had avoided the possibility of having a part-time student assistance counselor brought in from a community agency who might have been in direct competition with them for funding and support. I was on their team. They, too, gave me a list of students and parents they felt needed intervention. Plus Sue Ireland, who was cofacilitator for the peer counseling program with special education teacher Gail Angel, indicated that perhaps I could help with training student peer counselors.

As part of the process of meeting with the counselors, I also met with the guidance secretaries, Kathy Holden and Gail Palasek. I indicated to them that I would be planning a weekly calendar of students whom I wanted to see in individual and groups counseling and asked their input on the best way to send passes to these students so they could attend the sessions. I also asked their input on referring any student or parent who they thought seemed troubled. They observed hundreds of students each day and were positioned to sense a potential problem. I was beginning to get a sense of how to proceed already with a list of students who might need counseling, groups I could facilitate with Lorraine, and being involved in training students as helpers with Sue and Gail.

As August proceeded, I kept my outreach in full gear. I wanted to be ready and set with a tentative program by the end of the month. I met with Mike Wallace, one of the teachers from the school's alternative education program, who said he was excited that I would counsel students and parents in the program. There were approximately twenty students enrolled in the program from grades ten through twelve. Many of the students had academic, personal, and health problems. Mike suggested that I consider running two helping groups each week that would help the students resolve problems. He also recommended that I plan to see each student in individual counseling and make an effort to involve the parents, who were often hard to reach and leery of schools in general. Mike also recommended that he and I explore the possibility of connecting with the Board of Cooperative Educational Services, a state agency that provided career training and alternative graduation paths for marginal students from area schools, to explore a connection to help students graduate on time.

I also met with Jim Casey, the teacher of the school's leadership class. Jim reported the class was made up of approximately twenty-five eleventh-grade students who were selected because of their leadership skills. The class met each day and the students received full credit toward graduation. In class, the students were taught leadership skills and also regularly visited the district's three elementary schools to educate students about the risks involved in abusing alcohol along with other health issues. The students also were required to maintain a weekly journal of their experiences and meet for one-on-one supervision with Jim. He suggested that I plan to come into the class on a regular basis to train students in how to be effective helpers and also how they, as leaders, could include peers who were different in terms of color, culture, ability, economics, and family life. Jim reported that one of the initial problems that he faced with students was that their vision of leadership was telling people what to do rather than involving them as partners in the process and including those who seemed resistant. Perhaps I could help him to train students in this inclusion process.

Jim also reported that students were asked to sign a pledge that they would not use alcohol or drugs while in the class. Sometimes, he said, this led to complications for some class members. He also recommended that I see some of these students in individual counseling sessions because they were high achievers with many pressures and responsibilities. He gave me a list of incoming students and described the problems he knew some of them were experiencing. My individual and group counseling list was growing by the day, as were my training opportunities. This was fun and exciting, building a part of the intervention process based on real needs from the ground up rather than simply adding an additional layer of information, such as assemblies, from the top down.

Next on my list was parent leader Ann Brezolla. Ann had two children at the high school and was very involved in advocating for more parent education and involvement at the school. Ann had been in my parent training workshop at the middle school so we had a working relationship. She supported my observation that we needed to educate parents about the realities of teen life, to move them from their dreamy notion that their children would be problem free if their parents provided them with the proper guidance, nutrition, and supervision, and also provide the parents with the necessary skills to handle and resolve conflicts that are sure to arise in teen–parent relationships. Ann particularly stressed that parent education include a systematic outreach to parents who were at the margins of school–community life.

We needed to develop a process to educate these marginal parents that the school wanted their involvement and contributions and that the school belonged to them as much as to any other parent group. As a part of this process we needed to educate the so-called inner circle of parent leaders in how to include and value these marginal parents, not simply see them as losers who were raising troubled kids. Ann also suggested that the parent group would be interested in conducting a series of school–community forums on topics related to student health and well-being. She cited a wave of auto-related injuries suffered by students on weekends and cases of vandalized property. As we talked we both came up with a label for such forums as well as a plan of action. TALK would be a series for forums jointly planned by parents, students, interested educators, community members, and community law enforcement, recreation, health and mental health agencies.

In the final weeks before school I met with athletic director and physical education teacher Mike Schwenk. Mike was a progressive educator in the model of Naperville's Phil Lawler. In our conversation, he indicated an interest in offering special training, such as Project Adventure, for students in the alternative education program, and serving as a sounding board on how I should proceed to involve students in health-issue groups that would help students stop or reduce smoking, stay sober on weekends, and deal with eating disorders. I also met with social studies teachers Kevin Mann and Mike Minor and special education teacher Beverly Didie, who were members of the teacher advisor committee. They suggested that I come aboard as a member of the committee to help plan a training program for advisors similar to the one that I had developed at the middle school.

Last on my list was assistant principal Tom Heinegg, who handled the school's discipline problems. Tom was also new to the school and was looking for more proactive ways to help students who were in a revolving door of acting-out behaviors, such as tobacco smoking, suspensions, and returning to school and then being suspended again.

He noted that interventions such as speakers at assemblies and sharing of horror stories about addictions were good publicity for the school but did little to steer students in more positive directions. I told him about my conversations with nurse Esper about offering groups to help students stop or reduce smoking, stay sober on weekends, and deal with eating disorders, as well as my involvement with the leadership class, alternative school, parent education, and the like. Tom agreed to give me support, such as release time for Lorraine Esper so she could colead groups. He said he was growing tired of being in a reactive role, dishing out discipline to students with little apparent change in their marginal behavior. He suggested that I consider offering a mandatory counseling group and individual counseling for students who were being disciplined for using alcohol and drugs at school functions, required participation that would be offered as an alternative to suspension and perhaps, in some cases, that would open up the possibility of referral to rehab. Tom provided me with a list of marginal students and parents whom he saw on a regular basis, as well as a list of high-achieving students who, while successful in school, were rumored to be involved in risky behaviors on weekends.

By the end of August my conversations with various members of the school's intervention team had yielded many suggestions that could be translated into a weekly intervention program with specific components. Here is how I planned my week:

1. Individual counseling. I had a potential individual counseling list from Ray McGagli, Lorraine Esper, Jim Casey, Mike Wallace, Tom Heinegg, and counselors Jim Sheridan, Sue Ireland, and Kelly Young.
2. Group counseling. I had group counseling themes that might prove attractive to students, such as voluntary participation in groups to stop or reduce smoking, stay sober on weekends, and get help for eating disorders. I also was prepared to offer two groups for members of the alternative high school. Finally, I was prepared to offer a mandatory counseling group, as well as individual counseling for students who abused alcohol or drugs at a school function, as an alternative to suspension and a possible pathway to rehab.
3. Parent training. I needed to set aside time to meet with parent leaders on possible workshops and forums.
4. Training. I also needed to set specific times to meet on a regular basis with the leadership class, train peer counselors, and be involved in possible advisor training.
5. Membership in CST and KIN. I needed to prepare myself to contribute to both CST and KIN meetings that were held once a week.
6. Visibility. I had to make time to be out among the students, staff, and parents. I had to be visible and known, and to establish a welcoming, trusting atmosphere. That meant greeting and talking with students as they came to school, standing outside my office between periods to greet students and invite them in for conversation that might lead to counseling, walking the halls and talking with students, again inviting them to visit my office and talk, visiting the faculty rooms for teacher input, conversing with support staff and office secretaries to get their observations, visiting the offices of the school nurse and assistant principal to observe what was happening, sharing lunch with students and staff, and attending athletic and art, music, and drama events.
7. And finally, I would meet weekly with principal Norman Bussiere and assistant principal Tom Heinegg to keep them up to date on my progress and get their input.

When the school year began in September 1988, I was ready and set thanks to the openness, advice, and support of fellow intervention team members, who had shown me a path that I could follow to be helpful and useful. This big boost gave me a head start and by June I had seen over 300 of the schools, 750 students in individual and group counseling. I had offered mandatory group and individual counseling for students who abused alcohol and drugs at school functions; referred students for rehab and coordinated their reentry to school; begun a parent education program and made plans for TALK forums; become a regular part of the alternative education program, CST, and KIN; offered training and counseling for leadership class members; and connected with BOCES to offer GED training for alternative education students. I found my niche and filled a niche in the school's intervention program. My training at the middle school in counseling, training, and program development paid off, as did my ability to listen and build a program component based on what was needed in the school.

Over the next few years Ann Brezolla and I developed a series of school–community forums; the members of the teacher advisor committee and I developed a training program for advisors; and nurse Esper and I developed a tobacco intervention group using reformed smokers as coleaders. This last program gained national recognition and is described in my book *What Schools Should Do to Help Kids Stop Smoking.*[10]

However, as in most high schools, crises involving students, parents, and teachers continued to occur. The tragic death of Coach Lennon in 1992 rocked the school community, but, as reported earlier, the intervention team was ready and set. Under the leadership of principal Tom Heinegg, formerly the assistant principal, the team acted in a very coordinated and professional manner. Tom had in place a crisis plan for such an event and modeled caring and helping behaviors. Ray McGagli, nurse Esper, the three guidance counselors, and I counseled members of the team, student body, faculty, and parents. Teacher advisors used their sessions to address student concerns. Student peer counselors led by Gail Angle and Sue Ireland placed themselves throughout the school to offer help. There were many open doors for help. And there existed the necessary commitment of leadership, collaboration, professional development, personnel, time, and funding, and enhanced communication advocated by Floretta Dukes McKenzie and Julius Richmond to meet the challenges of making coordinated school health programs a reality.

I believe the intervention team had an additional, special advantage. They did not let issues of turf, rank, areas of expertise, or years of experience interfere with the necessary work needed to help students, parents, and staff. The focus of the team was on delivering help in as timely and efficient a manner as possible and involving as many members of the team as was necessary. They understood that each team member had a unique role and contribution that if ignored or devalued would lessen the overall strength of the team.

In closing let me say that the major focus of this book, the need to provide many open doors of help for students and parents, is a reflection of my own personal and professional persona, experience, and journey. The move to the high school, with all its seeming drawbacks, proved to be an open door through which I could pass to further my own personal and professional development, so that in the process I could offer the same kind of support I was receiving to the students and parents who were experiencing similar feelings of self-doubt, low self-esteem, and being at the margins of the school community that I felt in June 1987. As the old expression goes, "It takes one to know one." Or better said, it is useful for helpers to be aware of their own setbacks and troubles in trying to make connections with students. We are more coupled than different.

NOTES

1. Centers for Disease Control and Prevention (CDC), *Stories from the Field: Lessons Learned about Building Coordinated School Health Programs* (Atlanta: Centers for Disease Control and Prevention, 2003), xxi, 1–3.

2. William L. Fibkins, *The Empowering School* (San Jose, Calif.: Resource Publications, 1995).

3. Carnegie Council on Adolescent Development, *Turning Points: Preparing American Youth for the 21st Century* (New York: Carnegie Corporation, 1989).

4. National Commission of Excellence in Education, *A Nation at Risk* (Washington: U.S. Department of Education, 1983), d18–26.

5. Arthur G. Powell, Eleanor Farrar, and David Cohen, *The Shopping Mall High School* (Boston: Houghton Mifflin, 1985), 8–9, 34–37, 46–49, 86, 91, 268–269, 318.

6. Steve Farkas, and Jean Johnson, "Kids These Days: What Americans Really Think about the Next Generation," *Public Agenda* (1997): 8, 9, 11, 13, 16–19, 25–26.

7. National Association of Secondary School Principals (NASSP), *Executive Summary of Breaking Ranks 11: Strategies for Leading High School Reform* (Reston, Va.: NASSP, 2004), 1–6.

8. Floretta Dukes McKenzie, and Julius B. Richmond, "Linking Health and Learning: An Overview of Coordinated School Health Programs," in *Health Is Academic*, eds. Eva Marx and Susan Frelick Wooley (New York: Teachers College Press, 1998), 8–9.

9. Howard Adelman, "School Counseling, Psychological, and Social Services," in *Health Is Academic*, eds. Eva Marx and Susan Frelick Wooley (New York: Teachers College Press, 1998), 152–153.

10. William L. Fibkins, *What Schools Should Do to Help Kids Stop Smoking* (Larchmont, NY: Eye on Education, 2000), 132–139.

References

Adelman, Howard. "School Counseling, Psychological, and Social Services." In Eva Marx and Susan Frelick Wooley (Eds.), *Health Is Academic: A Guide to Coordinated School Health Programs.* New York: Teachers College Press, 1998.

Ahl, Carolyn. "Helping At-Risk Kids Get 'Teen Smart.'" minoritynurse.com, 27 January 2002. www.minoritynurse.com/features/undergraduate/01/27/02g .html (accessed 10 May 2004).

American School Counselor Association (ASCA). (2002). *Executive Summary of the ASCA National Model: A Framework for School Counseling Programs.* Alexandria, Va.: American School Counselor Association.

Association for Supervision and Curriculum Development (ASCD). (Fall 1999). "The Counselor's Role." *ASCD Curriculum Update.*

Association for Supervision and Curriculum Development (ASCD). (Fall 1999). "Schools as Communities." *ASCD Curriculum Update.*

Austin, Elizabeth. "Profile of Lisa Beckman." *Advances 3.* Princeton, NJ: Robert Wood Johnson Foundation, 2000, 4.

Bernard, Bonnie. "Fostering Resiliency in Kids." *Educational Leadership 51*(3) (November 1993). www.ascd.org/readingroom/edlead.9311.bernard.html (accessed 7 June 2003).

Blythe, William. "All the Children Are above Average." *New York Times*, (14 March 2004): 6, 7.

Bowers, Judy L., and Patricia A. Hatch. (2002). *The ASCA National Model for School Counseling Programs.* Alexandria, Va.: American School Counselor Association, 7–9.

Brackett, Elizabeth. "Fit for Life." PBS Interview, March 22, 2002. www.pbs.org/ newshour/bb/education/jan-june–2/pe_3–22.html (accessed 27 March 2002).

185

Carnegie Council on Adolescent Development. (1989). *Turning Points: Preparing American Youth for the 21st Century*. New York: Carnegie Corporation.

Centers for Disease Control and Prevention (CDC). (2003). *Stories from the Field: Lessons Learned about Building Coordinated School Health Programs*. Atlanta: Centers for Disease Control and Prevention, xxi, 1–3.

Checkley, Kathy. "Emphasizing Skills and Prevention to Form a More Health-Literate People." Association for Supervision and Curriculum Development (ASCD), Health Education Update, Spring 2000. www.ascd.org/readingroom/cupdate/2000/1spring00.html (accessed 7 April 2002).

"Comprehensive Bill to Truly Leave No Child Behind." Unveiling of Dodd-Miller Act 2003. www.cdfactioncouncil/org/ALNCB_reintroduction_PR.html (accessed 6 March 2004).

Conant, James B. (1959). *The American High School Today*. New York: McGraw Hill.

Cook, David R. (1971). "The Future of Guidance as a Profession." In David R. Cook (Ed.), *Guidance for Education in Revolution*. Boston: Houghton Mifflin.

Cormier, Ryan. "School Sued over Teen's Suicide: Parents Fault Abandonment on Field Trip." *Newsday*, 21 July 2000 (accessed 16 March 2004 via Suffolk County, New York, Cooperative Library System).

Davenport, Christine. "Student Obesity Targeted." washingtonpost.com, 11 February 2004, B05. www.washingtonpost.com/ac2/wp-dyn/A30235–2004Feb10?language=printer (accessed 11 March 2004).

Dryfoos, Joy. "The Mind-Body-Building Equation." *Educational Leadership* 57(6) (March 2000). www.ascd.org/readingroom/edlead.2003.dryfoos.html (accessed 7 April 2002).

Eagan, Timothy. "Body-Conscious Boys Adapt Athletes' Taste for Steroids." *New York Times*, (22 November 2002): 1, 24 (A).

Ebert, Roger. "The Perfect Score." *Chicago Sun-Times* 2004. www.suntimes.com/egibin/print.cgi (accessed 2 August 2004).

Erard, Michael. "Where to Get a Good Idea: Steal It Outside Your Group." newyorktimes.com, 22 May 2004. www.nytimes.com/2004/05/22/arts/22IDEA.html (accessed 28 May 2004).

Farkas, Steve, and Jean Johnson. "Kids These Days: What Americans Really Think about the Next Generation." *Public Agenda* (1997): 8–9, 11, 13, 16–19, 25–26.

Fibkins, William L. "Combating Student Tobacco Addiction in Secondary Schools." *National Association of Secondary School Principals (NASSP) Bulletin* 77(557) (December 1993): 51–59.

Fibkins, William L. (1995). *The Empowering School*. San Jose, Calif.: Resource Publications.

Fibkins, William L. "When a Beloved Teacher and Coach Dies." *National Association of Secondary School Principals (NASSP) Bulletin 82*(597) (July 1998): 88–93.

Fibkins, William L. (2000). *What Schools Should Do to Help Kids Stop Smoking*. Larchmont, NY: Eye on Education.

Fibkins, William L. (2002). *An Administrator's Guide to Better Teacher Mentoring*. Lanham, MD: Scarecrow Press.

Fibkins, William L. (2003). *An Educator's Guide to Understanding the Personal Side of Students' Lives*. Lanham, MD: Scarecrow Press.

Fowler-Finn, Thomas. (2003). "Profile." In Michael Sadowski (Ed.), *Adolescents at School: Perspective on Youth, Identity, and Education*. Boston: Harvard Education Press.

Frank. "The Lost Children of Rockdale County." PBS *Frontline* Interview, 2003. www.pbs.org/wgbh/pages/frontline/shows/Georgia/interviews/frank.html (accessed 13 March 2004).

Frey, Darcy. "Betrayed by the Game." *New York Times Magazine*, (15 February 2004): 14, 16, 18–19 (6).

Galley, Michelle. "Student Self-Harm: Silent School Crisis." *Education Week*, 2003. www.edweek.org.ew/ewstory.cfm?slug=14Cutters.h23 (accessed 14 January 2004).

Gewertz, Catherine. "Trusting School Community Linked to Student Gains." *Education Week*, 2003. www.edweek.org/ew/ewstory.cfm?slug=07trust.h22 (accessed14 January 2004).

Goode, Erica. "Stronger Warning Is Urged on Antidepressants for Teenagers." *New York Times*, (3 February 2004): 12 (A).

Hampel, Robert. (1986). *The Last Citadel*. Boston: Houghton Mifflin.

Harris-Bowman, Darcia. "Health Care Hub." *Education Week*, 4 February 2004. www.edweek.org/_printstory.cfm?slug+21HealthCenter.h23 (accessed 2 June 2004).

Healy, Patrick. "2 L. I. Coaches in Hazing Case Are Removed from Teaching." *New York Times*, (25 March 2004):5 (B).

Herszenhorn, David M. "Broad Overhaul in New York City to Replace Many Middle Schools." *New York Times*, (3 March 2004): 1, 6 (B).

Hollywood.com. "Prozac Nation." Hollywood.com 2004. www.hollywood.com/movies/details/movies/376226 (accessed 28 July 2004).

Hulbert, Ann. "Are the Kids All Right?" *New York Times Magazine*, (11 April 2004): 9–10 (6).

Hurst, Marianne D. "Columbine High: Five Years Later." *Education Week*, 14 April 2004. www.edweek.org/ewstory.cfm?slug=31cp;umbine.h23 (accessed 20 April 2004).

Jacobson, Steve. "Mepham: Can Any Good Come of It?" *Newsday*, (18 January 2004): 31 (B).

Jacobson, Steve. "Mepham Divided: Victims, Villains." *Newsday*, (26 October 2003): 35 (B).

Levine, Eliot. "One Kid at a Time." *Educational Leadership 59*(7) (April 2002): 29–32.

Levine, Meredith. "Tell the Doctor All Your Problems But Keep It to Less Than a Minute." *New York Times*, (1 June 2004): 6 (F).

Lightfoot, Cynthia. (1997). *The Culture of Adolescent Risk-Taking*. New York: The Guilford Press.

Longman, Jere. "An Athlete's Dangerous Experiment." *New York Times*, (26 November 2003): 1, 4 (D).

McKenna, Margaret A. "Columbine Leaves Many Lessons Behind." *Newsday*, (21 April 2004): 45 (A).

McKenzie, Floretta Dukes, and Julius B. Richmond. (1998). "Linking Health and Learning: An Overview of Coordinated School Health Programs." In Eva Marx and Susan Frelick Wooly (Eds.), *Health Is Academic: A Guide to Coordinated School Health Programs*. New York: Teachers College Press.

McMenamin, Brigid. "Turning to Tutors Instead of Schools." *New York Times*, (26 October 2003): 5 (BU).

Mitchell, Elvis. "'Normal' High School on the Verge." *New York Times*, (10 October 2003): 1, 24 (E).

Mitchell, Elvis. "Trading Barbie for Drugs, Sex, and Halter Tops." *New York Times*, (20 August 2003): 1, 5 (E).

Morris, Bonnie Rothman. "Letters on Students' Weight Ruffle Parents." *New York Times*, (26 March 2002): 7 (F).

Morris, Keiko, and Karla Schuster. "Appalled and Sickened." *Newsday*, (11 March 2004): 2–3, 59 (A).

Morris, Keiko, and Karla Schuster. "Coaches on Defense." *Newsday*, (31 March 2004): 2, 53 (A).

Mui, Ylan Q. "Scandals Stun Howard County in Academic Year Gone Sour." washingtonpost.com, 2004. www.washingtonpost.com/ac2?wp-dyn?A24026–2004 Feb8?language=printer (accessed 2 June 2004).

Munson, Harold. (1971). "Guidance in Secondary Education: Reconnaissance and Renewal." In David R. Cook (Ed.), *Guidance for Education in Revolution*. Boston: Allyn & Bacon.

National Association of Secondary School Principals (NASSP). (2004). *Executive Summary of Breaking Rules 11: Strategies for Leading High School Reform*. Reston, Va.: National Association of Secondary School Principals.

National Center for Education Statistics (NCES). "Principals' Perception of Discipline Issues in Their Schools." National Center for Education Statistics 1996–1997, www.nces.edgov/pubs98/violence/98030007.html (accessed 3 August 2002).

National Commission on Excellence in Education. (1983). *A Nation at Risk.* Washington, D.C.: U.S. Department of Education.

Noguera, Pedro A. "Special Topics: Transforming High Schools." *Education Leadership 61*(9) (May 2004). www.ascd.org/publications/edlead/200405/noguero.html (accessed 6 April 2004).

Pappano, Laura. "In ADH Debate, No Right Answers." Boston.com 2004. www.boston.com/news.education/K_12/articles/2004/03/07/in_adhd_debate-no_right_answer (accessed 8 March 2004).

Pennington, Bill. "As Team Sports Conflict, Some Parents Rebel." *New York Times Magazine,* (12 November 2003): 1, 7 (D).

Powell, Arthur D., Eleanor Farrar, and David Cohen. (1985). *The Shopping Mall High School.* Boston: Houghton Mifflin.

Pradnya, Joshi. "Riverhead Teenager's Suicide Prompts Law." *Newsday,* 13 July 2001 (accessed 16 March 2004 via Suffolk County, New York, Cooperative Library System).

Prose, Francine. "Close to Home." *New York Times,* (23 August 1992): 1, 21–22 (7).

Rasmussen, Karen. "Healthy Students, Staff, and Communities." Association for Supervision and Curriculum Development (ASCD), *Curriculum Update,* Fall 1999. www.ascd.org/readingroom/cupdate/1999/ifall/html (accessed 7 April 2004).

Reese, Shelly. "The Counselor's Conundrum: Provide Triage or Full-Service Programs." *Middle Ground,* (October 1998): 17–19, 24.

Resnick, Michael D. "Adrift in America: The Lost Children of Rockdale County." PBS *Frontline* Interview 2003. www.pbs.org/wgbh/pages/frontline/shows/georgia/isolated/resnick/html (accessed 11 March 2004).

Richardson, Virginia, and Patricia Colfer. (1990). "Being At-Risk in School." In John I. Goodlad and Pamela Keating (Eds.), *Access to Knowledge: An Agenda for Our Nation's Schools.* New York: College Entrance Board.

Ross, Beth. "The Lost Children of Rockdale County." PBS *Frontline* Interview 2003. www.pbs.org/wgbh/pages/frontline/shows/georgia/interviews/beth.html (accessed 11 March 2004).

Rothstein, Richard. "A Mobile Clinic Delivers Good Health and Grades." *New York Times,* (11 September 2002): 8 (B).

Sachem (NY) North High School. "Guidance." Sachem North High School website, 2003–2004. www.sachem.edu/schools/north/guidance2003_2004/index/html (accessed 26 February 2004).

Sanders, Lisa. "Diagnosis." *New York Times Magazine*, (21 September 2003): 24 (6).

Santora, Marc. "Case Tries to Link a Mother to Her Boy's Suicide." *New York Times*, (27 September 2003): 1, 6 (B).

Scardamaglia, Richard. "Teachers as Student Advocates." *Educational Leadership 50*(4) (December 1992–January 2003): 31–33.

Scherer, Marge. "Perspectives: Connected at the Roots." *Educational Leadership 61*(9) (May 2004). www.ascd.org/publications/ed_lead/200405/scherer.html (accessed 6 April 2004).

Schuster, Karla. "Keeping Pride Alive." *Newsday*, (26 October 2003): 3 16 (A).

Simmons, Roberta G., and Dale A. Blyth. (1987). *Moving into Adolescence: The Impact of Puberty Changes and School Context*. New York: Aldine De Gruyter.

Sinclair, Robert L., and Ward J. Ghory. (1990). "Last Things First: Realizing Equality by Improving Conditions for Marginal Students." In John I. Goodlad and Pamela Keating (Eds.), *Access to Knowledge: An Agenda for Our Nation's Schools*. New York: College Entrance Board.

Sirotnik, Kenneth A. (1990). "Equal Access to Quality in Public Schooling: Issues in the Assessment of Equity and Excellence." In John I. Goodlad and Pamela Keating (Eds.), *Access to Knowledge: An Agenda for Our Nation's Schools*. New York: College Entrance Board.

Smith, Carla. "A Model of Leadership." National Association of Secondary School Principals, principals.org, January 2004. www.nassp.org/publications/plpl_model-leadership_0104.cfm (accessed 13 January 2004).

Stack, Joetta L. "Riley Says It's Time to Rethink High Schools." *Education Week*, (22 September 2002): 20.

Staresina, Lisa N. "Student Mobility." *Education Week*, 2003, www.edweek.org/context/topics/issuespage.cfm_id=82 (accessed 14 January 2004).

Steinberg, Dan. "When You Get a Good Kid . . . It's Sad." washingtonpost.com, 29 May 2004. www.washingtonpost.com/ac2/wp-dyn/A64417–2004May28?language=printer (accessed 30 May 2004).

Talbot, Margaret. "Play Date with Destiny." *New York Times Magazine*, (21 September 2003): 31–35, 52, 64, 82–83 (6).

Tomlinson, Janis. "A Changing Panorama." Association for Supervision and Curriculum Development (ASCD) *Infobrief 27*, May 1999. www.ascd.org/readingroom/infobrief/9905.html (accessed 7 April 2002).

Torgerson, Warren. (1958). *Theory and Methods of Scaling*. New York: Wiley.

Travers, Peter. "Elephant." rollingstone.com 2003. www.rollingstone.com/reviews/movies/review/asp?mid=2047649 (accessed 16 March 2004).

Tse, Tomoeh Murakami. "Recalling Boy's 'Zest for Life.'" *Newsday*, (8 October 2003): 30 (A).

Vitello, Paul. "Schooled in Overlooking Trouble." *Newsday*, (14 March 2004): 6, 45 (A).

Vuko, Evelyn Porreca. "Youth Movement: How to Put Exercise into Play." washingtonpost.com, 23 December 2003, C 10. www.washingtonpost.com/ac2/wp-dyn/A23125–2003Dec22?language=printer (accessed 11 March 2004).

Wager, Barbara Reis. "No More Suspensions: Creating a Shared Ethical Culture." *Educational Leadership 50*(4) (December 1992–January 1993): 34–37.

Walter, Philip. "Schools Say Counseling Efforts Are Improving." *The Virginia Pilot*, (18 September 1996): 1, 9 (A).

Wang, Margaret C., Maynard C. Reynolds, and Herbert J. Walberg. "Serving Students at the Margins." *Educational Leadership 52*(4) (December 1994–January 1995): 1–9.

Winter, Gregg. "Wooing the Counselor Raises Enrollments and Also Eyebrows." *New York Times*, (8 July 2004): 1, 18 (A).

Index

About the Author

William L. Fibkins is a writer, university professor, education consultant, and lecturer specializing in training school administrators, teacher leaders, and school counselors on how to develop school-based teacher training centers and student support services. His training programs also include leadership and peer counseling training for student leaders; drug, alcohol, and tobacco intervention for students on the road to addiction; and training parents as reliable sources of help and referral for students and parents headed toward the margins of school life.

Fibkins holds degrees in education, counselor education, and school administration from Syracuse University and the University of Massachusetts.

Fibkins's publications include *An Educator's Guide to Understanding the Personal Side of Students' Lives, An Administrator's Guide to Better Teacher Mentoring, What Schools Should Do to Help Kids Stop Smoking, The Empowering School,* and *The Teacher-As-Helper Training Manual.* He is also the author of numerous professional monographs on restructuring secondary schools, training teachers as advisors, restructuring secondary school guidance services, designing and implementing group counseling programs, and developing school-based health centers to address teen health issues.

Fibkins's in-school experience includes serving as founder and director of the Stony Brook University-Bay Shore Public Schools Teacher Training Center, director of teacher training for the Queens College-Louis Armstrong

Intermediate School, and founder of the student assistance counseling program at the Shoreham-Wading River, New York, school district as well as chair of the Curriculum Development Committee at Shoreham. His university experience includes teaching in the school administration program at Queens College, New York City, and the Counseling and Human Development program at Long Island University, C.W. Post Campus, Brookville, New York.

3 5282 00615 0638